making scrapbooks:

complete guide to preserving your treasured memories

Vanessa-Ann

Sterling Publishing Co., Inc. New York
A Sterling/Chapelle Book

chapelle ltd.

owner: Jo Packham

editor: Leslie Ridenour

designers: Joy Anckner, Sherry Ferrin, Holly Fuller, Sharon Ganske, Amber Hansen, Pauline Locke, Jo Packham, Jamie Pierce, and Rhonda Rainey

staff: Marie Barber, Malissa Boatwright, Kass Burchett, Rebecca Christensen, Marilyn Goff, Michael Hannah, Shirley Heslop, Holly Hollingsworth, Susan Jorgensen, Ginger Mikkelsen, Barbara Milburn, Linda Orton, Karmen Quinney, Cindy Rooks, and Cindy Stoeckl

photography: Kevin Dilley, photographer for Hazen Photography   **photography stylist:** Susan Laws

watercolor artist: Pauline Locke

acknowledgements: Several projects in this book were created with outstanding and innovative products developed by the following manufacturers: Fiskars and Personal Stamp Exchange. We would like to offer our sincere appreciation to these companies for the valuable support given in this ever changing industry of new ideas, concepts, designs, and products.

Library of Congress Cataloging-in-Publication Data

Vanessa-Ann.
    Making scrapbooks : complete guide to preserving your treasured
memories / Vanessa-Ann.
        p. cm.
    "A Sterling/Chapelle book."
    Includes index.
    ISBN 0-8069-9900-4
    1. Photograph albums.   2. Photographs--Conservation and restoration.
3. Paper work.   4. Scrapbooks.   I. Title.
TR465.V36 1998
771'.46--dc21   98-33672
                                            CIP

10 9 8 7

A Sterling/Chapelle Book

First paperback edition published in 1998 by
Sterling Publishing Company, Inc.
387 Park Avenue South, New York, N.Y. 10016
© 1998 Chapelle Limited
Distributed in Canada by Sterling Publishing
% Canadian Manda Group, One Atlantic Avenue, Suite 105
Toronto, Ontario, Canada M6K 3E7
Distributed in Great Britain and Europe by Cassell PLC
Wellington House, 125 Strand, London WC2R 0BB, England
Distributed in Australia by Capricorn Link (Australia) Pty Ltd.
P.O. Box 704, Windsor, NSW 2756, Australia
Printed in China
All rights reserved

Sterling ISBN 0-8069-9900-4 Trade
**   0-8069-9901-2 Paper**

If you have any questions or comments or would like information about any specialty products featured in this book, please contact:

Chapelle Ltd., Inc.
P.O. Box 9252
Ogden, UT 84409

Phone: (801) 621-2777
FAX: (801) 621-2788

contents

general information
scrapbooking 6
special techniques 14
archiving 18
family history 24
photography 27

interactive pop-up pictures

picture pop-up 30
baby bundle 33
happy birthday 34
daddy's coat 36
sunflower pocket 37
halloween 38
school lunch 39
holiday stocking 41

passion for pets
fold-out pets 43
pet pages 44–48
title page 45
critter quiz 45
pet profile 46
tradition 46
shane game 47

baby in black & white
baby book 49
baby pages 50–51
fabric photo mat 50
ribbon flowers 51
great-grandma 51

fabric through the year
seasons 52
valentine 54
bunny hop 55
pumpkin patch 56
pretty package 57

daughter's dreams

to my daughter 59
angel house 63
butterfly kisses 63
envelope keepers 65
family tree 66

highschool highlights
high school days 68
high school pages 69

weddings are forever
wedding album 76
wedding pages 77
weddings past 77
cordially invited 79
generations 79
poetry & lace 81
art of marriage 81
garter photo corners 82
victorian house 82

ribbon & lace
antiquity 85
family quilt 86
organdy envelope 88
wedding vows 90
grandma's fan 91
fushia frames 93
trellis 94
sister's favorite 95

textured treasures
days gone by 96
textured pages 97–107
little sister 98
pansy border 98
train 99
ship 100
dear friends 101
special delivery 102
oriental lace 103
mother & daughter 103

sentimental journey
sentimental pages 108

other covers & bindings
angel cover 111
celestial insights cover . . . 112
simple appliqué cover 113
home sweet binding 115
string binding 115
flutter binding 117
receipt book binding 118
flower paper binding 119

scrapbook alternatives
japanese cookbook 120
treasure box 121
special awards 121
memories shadow box 124
framed box 125
flower girl 126
stamped envelope 127

metric conversion chart . 127
index 128

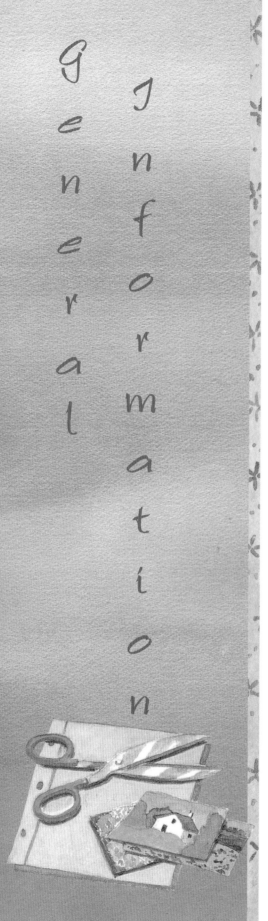

scrapbooking

introduction

Creating scrapbooks or photo albums is a means of preserving and protecting memories and a personal or family history. This book is meant to be a complete guide to products, supplies, and techniques that are currently available and in use for creatively compiling these treasured histories. Several special techniques that are not yet widely used are also presented as ideas for creating truly uncommon scrapbook covers and pages. These techniques incorporate interactive pop-up pages, découpage, fabric backgrounds, embossed metal, ribbon embroidery embellishment, hand-tinted photographs, marbled and sponged paper, and much more for showcasing precious photographs and memorabilia.

motivation

"Scrapbooking" is a hobby that not only provides a creative outlet for the scrapbook designer, but also promotes a strong sense of self-esteem and belonging for those whose life and accomplishments are creatively chronicled and compiled into an album or collection of albums. By employing a little planning and basic know-how, the end result will be a link between past, present, and future as these memory books remain for generations to come.

calculating page measurements

Most instructions for covers and pages in this book do not contain exact measurements due to the fact that there are so many different sizes of scrapbooks and pages available. To figure reduction and enlargement percentages for provided patterns, use the following formulas:

Larger Desired Size ÷ Actual Size = Enlargement %
Example: 11" ÷ 7.5" = 1.4 (140%)

Smaller Desired Size ÷ Actual Size = Reduction %
Example: 4" ÷ 7.5" = .53 (53%)

Measure for both height and width and choose the smaller percentage to fit all within desired size page or area.

beginning with safe photograph handling, a theme, and a color scheme

Tackling drawers and shoe boxes full of photographs can be overwhelming. Begin by setting aside a work space in the home that can be left with scrapbook supplies out in the open for easy and regular access and will not be disturbed.

Wash hands throroughly before handling photographs. Natural oils from skin can be harmful to photographs, so even clean hands must be washed frequently while working on scrapbooks. When possible, try to handle photographs by the edges.

Create a sort of filing system by designating and labeling one or more file folders or photo boxes for each member of the family and one to represent the whole family. Organize photographs and memorabilia chronologically (by year or decade) and by family member into the file folders or photo boxes.

After sorting photographs, use a photo labeling pencil to identify the who, what, where, when, how, and why of each photo in each folder or box. Write on the back top or edges of the photo. These inexpensive, photo-safe pencils are available at any photography supply store. Many varieties of labeling pencils can be used to safely write on both front or back of a photograph and will wipe off with a tissue. Do not use a ball point, felt tip, or water based pen to label photo-

graphs. These pens may create indentation lines on the photograph's face and their inks may eventually bleed through, becoming visible on the face of the photograph.

photo labeling pencil **ballpoint & felt tip pens**

Employ the knowledge of friends and family members to help identify dates, people, places, and events pictured (a family reunion or gathering is a good place to find such help).

It is recommended to have at least one album for each family member and another to represent the whole family. Choose a scrapbook album that allows for the greatest amount of flexibility and creativity. Album bindings should allow pages to lie flat.

Begin crafting scrapbook pages by putting most recent photographs into albums first and staying current as new memories are made. Film should be developed and photographs should be printed and labeled as soon as possible. As these are kept up to date, there will be time to place older photographs and memorabilia in albums. Remember to handle photographs, when placing them on scrapbook pages, with the same amount of care as was taken at the time of organizing them. Keep glues and other adhesives off the face of photos. Even stickers placed over the face of a photograph can leave sticky residue that may be difficult to remove.

For each page, choose two to four photos, a theme, and a color scheme. Be selective when choosing and mounting photographs. They should be well-focused, interesting, and varied.

Many photographs suggest a theme or represent a special event. For example, a photograph of a child blowing out candles on a birthday cake will be used to build a page with a birthday theme. Decide what kind of emotion or mood is reflected by the theme and use it as a guide when choosing scrapbook page patterns and accents.

Add color to scrapbook pages by using complementary colored paper products, pens, markers, and more. Use colors that traditionally represent the theme of the scrapbook page. For example, keep with bright and pastel colors—not neutral and earth colors—to design a Spring page. Choose colors that reinforce and enhance the page's theme, not detract from it.

Finally, use a few of the many available scrapbook supplies to accentuate the photographs, theme, and colors to build scrapbook pages that are both attractive and long lasting. *See **Archiving** on pages 18–24 for valuable information on creating and preserving scrapbooks.*

choosing from available scrapbook supplies

It is not necessary to own every scrapbooking item on the market to begin creating scrapbook pages. The must-haves are: an acid free album; mounting papers; adhesives; paper; water- and fade-proof pens, pencils, and markers; craft scissors; photos; and time. Begin with these basics and as interest grows, so will a collection of fun-to-have supplies. The following is a listing of the many available supplies that can be used for designing and creating scrapbook pages.

adhesives: include acid free double stick photo tape and stickers, glue sticks, neutral pH adhesive, and two-way glue.

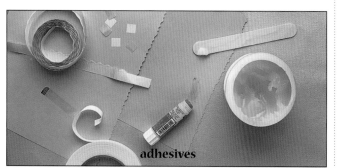
adhesives

albums & binders: are available in all sizes, colors, styles, and formats. The main difference between scrapbooks is in the binding. Choose from three-ring binders, expandable binders, and bound scrapbooks.

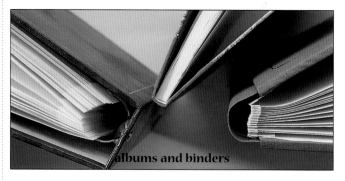
albums and binders

circle cutter: This tool adjusts to the desired diameter of the circle. It makes a perfectly clean circular cut.

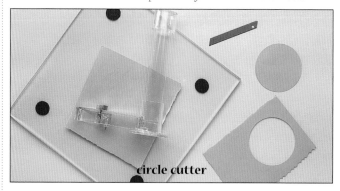
circle cutter

clip art: Lined art images are available in booklets to copy and cut to accent scrapbook pages. Clip art is also available in the form of computer software and can be printed to paper and cut out for quick and easy page decorations.

color wheel: This tool is a visual representation of the spectrum of colors in the shape of a wheel. When choosing colors, select a primary color and use the wheel to choose complementary colors.

color wheel
clip art

corner rounders: are similar in appearance to craft punches. They trim square corners off photographs and papers, leaving curved corners.

corner templates: are used to trim corners on photographs and papers into shapes. Position clear acrylic templates over item to be trimmed, trace shape, and cut. Use a photo labeling pencil when tracing to a photograph as any remnant tracing will wipe off with a tissue.

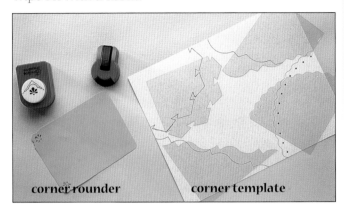

corner rounder   **corner template**

craft knife: A knife with a replaceable blade makes cutting straight edges and tight corners clean and easy.

craft punches: are available in several sizes and motifs, from hearts to dinosaurs, stars to palm trees, and more. These are used to punch colored paper or cardstock for small shapes to enhance a page.

craft scissors: Dedicate a good pair of scissors for cutting paper and other craft items.

craft knife

craft punch   **craft scissors**

crimper/corrugator: corrugates papers and cards adding dimension and texture to a page.

decorative edge scissors: Use these fun scissors to cut colored papers and photographs with distinctive edges. There are several different edges to choose from to accent any theme.

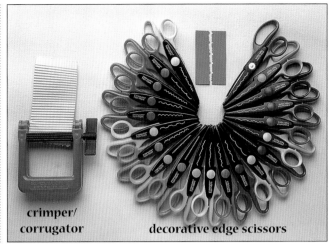

crimper/ corrugator   **decorative edge scissors**

die cuts: are available in several colors and sizes. They are cut from varied weights of paper and are a quick way to add thematic shapes and colors to a page. Die cuts can be purchased individually or in theme packets. Many paper stores have a die cut machine that patrons can use to cut their own papers, to get both the shape and color they desire.

embossing stencils: These brass plates are available in several designs that can be gently pressed into scrapbook papers creating a raised effect.

embossing stencils

die cuts

lettering booklets: feature creative techniques of writing and decorating the alphabet. These booklets demonstrate how to complete styles such as dot, outline, and block lettering.

light box: available in varied sizes, these boxes have an acrylic top and a light enclosed within. Use them to transfer clip art or lettering designs directly to the scrapbook mounting page. Place the design, right side up, on a light box and the mounting page on top, right side up. Trace the design to the page. *Note: This technique can be duplicated by holding the design and mounting page up to a sunlit window.*

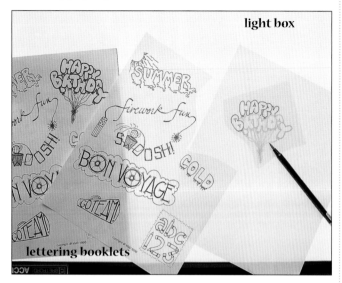

light box

lettering booklets

novelty edge rulers: are used to create a continuous pattern along one or more edges of a paper. Patterns include wavy, zigzag, scallop, and more. Position clear acrylic rulers on paper, trace pattern, and cut.

paper: adds dimension and color to a scrapbook. Cardstock is a heavier weight paper often used for mounting and creating die cuts and punched shapes. Decorative or novelty papers and stationery are often used for page backgrounds and to create patterns and borders .

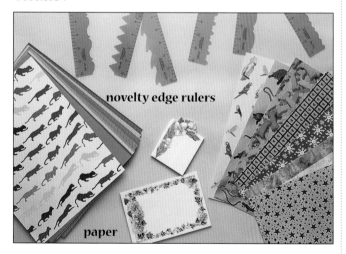

novelty edge rulers

paper

paper cutter & trimmers: Rotary paper cutters are used with a cutting mat to make straight cuts and square corners. Trimmers cut straighter than scissors.

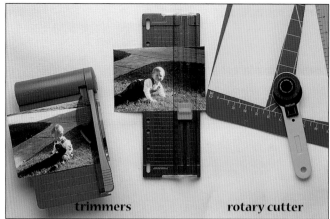

trimmers   rotary cutter

pens, pencils, & markers: Use these for labeling, highlighting, and captioning. Make certain pens and markers are fade proof, waterproof and use pigment ink. Pens are available in all colors and with several different tips such as .01 tip for creating fine lines, and tiny accents; .05 tip for standard clean lines; and a 45° angle for calligraphic effect for titles and special emphasis. Colored pencils that are water resistant and light fast can also be used to decorate scrapbook pages. Markers (often called brush markers) are also available in all colors and are used to color in traced or stamped motifs.

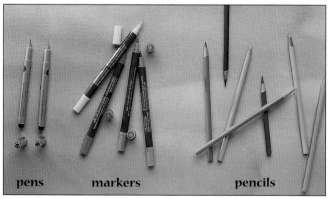

pens   markers   pencils

pH testing pen: instantly tests acid content of paper. *See **Finding Acid Free Scrapbook Supplies** on page 21.*

photo corners: allow for removal of photographs from scrapbooks. Use colored or transparent photo corners to mount very old or priceless photographs.

photo frames: are available in several colors. Embossed and of cardstock thickness, these can be used to mat studio portrait photographs. *See* ***Cropping Photographs*** *on page 12.*

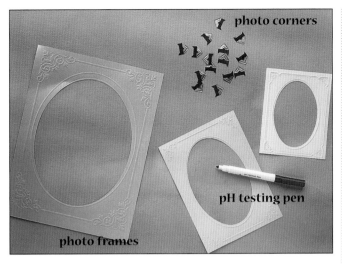

photo corners

pH testing pen

photo frames

rubber stamps, pigment ink pads,
embossing powders, heat tool

photo labeling pencil: used for recording information about the photograph and for tracing a stencil or template to a photograph. *See **Beginning with Safe Photograph Handling, a Theme, and a Color Scheme** on page 7 for photograph.*

red eye pen: fixes red eyes on photographs. The pen contains a dye that filters out the color red, allowing natural eye features to show through. *See **Correcting Red Eye** on page 28.*

red eye pen

rubber stamps, pigment ink pads, embossing powder, & heat tool: There are numerous individual rubber stamps, rubber stamp kits, and pigment ink pads available to use to enhance a scrapbook page. Color in the designs with pigment ink brush markers and/or apply colored embossing powder and set with a heat tool.

sheet protectors: Top loading, clear sheets are used in three-ring binders to hold two 8½" x 11" scrapbook pages back to back. Sheet protectors envelope the scrapbook pages and keep photographs on facing pages from rubbing together. They are also available with non-glare surfaces. *See **Plastic Terms** on page 19.*

spray neutralizer: To *safely* include high acid items in albums, spray them with a substance made specifically for deacidification. The spray coats the paper and neutralizes acid levels. The sprayed item should then be displayed on buffered paper. *See **Saving Non-archival Quality Memorabilia** on page 21.*

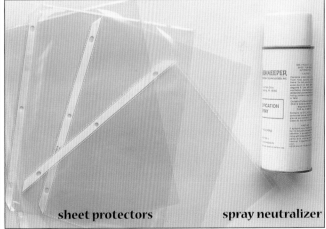

sheet protectors   spray neutralizer

stencils & templates: are used to trim photographs and papers into shapes such as hearts, circles, stars, balloons, etc. to eliminate unnecessary background or to match a theme. Cookie cutters work well as templates—they are available in all sizes and shapes and are easy to trace. Position templates over item to be trimmed, trace shape, and cut out. Use a photo labeling pencil when tracing to a photograph as any remnant tracing will wipe off with a tissue.

stickers: are available in all sorts of themes, sizes, and colors. They add instant color, humor, and artistic impact.

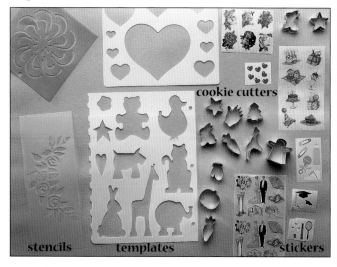

stencils   templates   cookie cutters   stickers

theme packets & kits: are assortments that often contain nearly everything (except photographs and pens) needed to create a themed page. Collections can include die cuts, stickers, cardstock, rubber stamps, background papers, stationery, and sheet protectors.

don'ts

The following items and practices should be avoided when compiling scrapbooks:

Ball point pen on photographs
Construction and crepe paper
Cutting instant photographs
Cutting very old or priceless photographs
Exposing scrapbooks to water, exhaust, humidity, insects, extreme heat, or direct light
Felt-tip and water-based pens
Fingerprints on photographs
Magnetic self-adhesive photo albums and pages
Masking tape
PVC (polyvinyl chloride) plastic
Rubber cement

Storing scrapbooks and photo negatives in the same location
Transparent tape

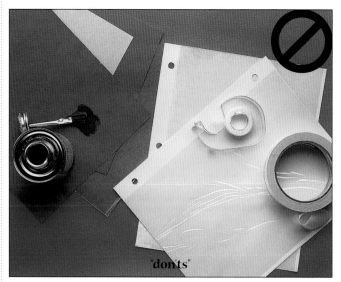

"don'ts"

cropping photographs

Many scrapbook designers will choose to crop, or cut, photographs to remove unwanted background, emphasizing the foreground or people, and to create fun shapes. Snapshots, which are often incorrectly framed at the time of photographing the subject, are candidates for cropping. This technique will not affect the stability of a photograph. Cropping is completely safe, but it is irreversible. Consider cropping color copies of irreplaceable one-of-a kind photographs. Cropping studio photographs is not recommended, since professional photographs are typically framed well, with little unnecessary background. Studio portraits can be framed with decorative paper cutouts or photo frames. NEVER crop an instant photograph. Make color copies of instant photographs. The color copies can then be cropped as desired and added to pages.

enhancements

This term refers to items used to dress up a scrapbook page and complement its photographs. Enhancements include die cuts, stickers, punched papers, and lettering. Remember, these are used to enhance the page, not overpower it. Be selective, stay with the theme of the page, and maintain balance.

photo journaling

Document photographs by either hand-writing or lettering names, dates, and events—again, the who, what, where, when, how, and why—on the scrapbook mounting page. Write personal feelings and humorous captions about the event. Include family stories, poems, and songs that correspond with the photograph. For a child's scrapbook, write down first words, favorite phrases, and any grammatical errors and manners of speech to capture the child's development over time. For example, a three-year-old child has difficulty pronouncing the letters "C" and "G" and always transposes them as "T" and "D." On a page where photographs show him playing his favorite game of tag, write the accompanying phrase, "You _tan't_ _det_ me!"

lettering

Lettering is the technique of creatively writing and decorating words, phrases, and titles. This technique makes the text an element of page design, drawing attention to the words. There are many different styles to choose from such as simple serifs, dot lettering, outline lettering, block lettering, and word pictures to match a theme. Write the words in the lettering style on the page in pencil first, then go over pencil with a pen or marker. Keep letter spacing even and consistent for a more unified appearance.

memorabilia—what to save

The purpose of crafting a scrapbook is to provide a place to keep "scraps." Tangible reminders of people, places, and events can include any of the following memorabilia. See **Saving Non-archival Quality Memorablia** on page 21.

Announcements
Autographs
Awards
Birth certificates, hospital bracelets, sonogram
   copies, etc.
Brochures
Certificates
Children's drawings

Greeting cards
Guest lists
Handprints
Letters
Locks of hair
Maps
Marriage licenses
Menus
Newspaper clippings
Obituaries
Post cards
Programs
Recipes
Report cards
Ribbons
Ticket stubs
Wedding invitations

pocket pages

To hold memorabilia separate from a photo page, create a pocket page by gluing two mounting pages together along bottom and both sides. Remember to cut a curve into the top edge of the top page for easy access to the contents of the pocket page.

organizing supplies

Organize file folders, which were used to sort photographs, in file cabinets or stackable file boxes. See **Beginning with Safe Photograph Handling, a Theme and a Color Scheme** on page 7. Organize memorabilia by year in an accordion file, labeling the pocket with the year and any other identifying information.

Keep items such as stickers, die cut shapes, punch shapes, papers, and scraps in zipper-type baggies with holes punched along one side of the bags or in clear 2" x 2" slide size, 3½" x 2½" sports card size, 4" x 6" photo size, or 8½" x 11" top loading protector sheets. Organize them by occasion and color and store them together in a 3-ring binder.

Tools such as pens, decorative edge scissors, etc. can be stored in clear, plastic, stackable drawers. Portable canvas bags with multiple pockets also prove useful for storing and carrying needed supplies.

Another versitle option for storing all supplies in one place is a roll-away utility cart with drawers. Roll the cart to any room in the house for easy access to supplies wherever scrapbooking will be done.

"crop"

This term is often used to refer to a gathering of friends on a set date, at a set time and place, to work together on individual scrapbooks and share supplies and ideas for pages. Scrapbookers often plan monthly get-togethers that last for several hours and include potluck style refreshments. The crop can be held in a scrapbooker's home or in a larger facility such as a church building. Sometimes a crop is the main event in a getaway weekend with family or friends.

special techniques

cutting metal

Use an old or inexpensive pair of scissors to cut light weight metals such as copper. Try to avoid short, jagged edges, by keeping the scissors deep in the cut. Do not withdraw the blades until the entire cut is completed.

découpage

This is a smooth, thin-bodied, water soluble adhesive that dries clear and is used to adhere and seal paper to project surfaces. Coat the surface of the paper with découpage adhesive. Carefully place paper on project surface. Press paper lightly with fingertips and smooth out any air bubbles, working from the center to the outside. Let dry. Following manufacturer's instructions, coat entire surface with découpage adhesive. Let dry.

coating the paper surface

pressing paper to project surface

coating entire surface

embossing copper

Place the copper, right side up, on a stack of paper. Using a tin tool, a ballpoint pen, or a pencil, emboss the pattern onto the copper. Creating the pattern on the copper right side up will result in indented embossing. Creating the pattern on the copper wrong side up will result in raised embossing. Going over the pattern several times will result in deeper lines and will make details stand out more. Wipe the copper with a soft cloth to remove pen or pencil marks.

embossing copper

embossing paper

Use an embossing stencil and stylus to make an impression on the backside of a piece of paper. Lay stencil on front side of paper and lightly tape stencil to paper. Turn stencil over so paper is on top and lightly tape to a light box. Using stylus, begin by pressing around edges of design from side to side or top to bottom. Gently but firmly press paper through the stencil to create a raised design. Avoid scrubbing the stylus across largers areas of the design as this may leave grooves in the paper. Because work is being done from the backside, the embossed design will be a reverse image of what is seen on the stencil front.

embossing paper

fusible appliqué

To appliqué fabric to scrapbook pages, use double-sided fusible web. Enlarge pattern from book as necessary. Trace pattern onto translucent tracing paper. Turn tracing paper over so pattern is visible in reverse. Place fusible web facing reverse side of pattern, paper side up. Trace pattern on paper side of fusible web.

Follow manufacturer's instructions to fuse the web to the motif fabrics.

Cut out pattern following pattern line.

Peel off the paper backing and fuse the fabric motifs to paper or background fabric.

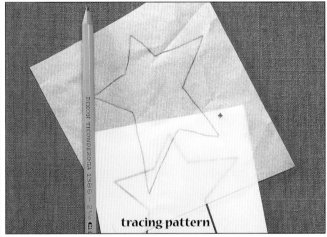
tracing pattern

fusing web to fabric

handmade paper ovals

Fill plastic dish pan full of water. Soak 11" x 15", 140 lb., acid free watercolor paper in dish pan for five minutes. Tear paper into dime-size pieces and soak for 30 additional minutes.

Fill blender two-thirds full of water. Drain paper and add to blender, one cup at a time. Blend on high speed.

Rinse dish pan and fill two-thirds full of water. Pour blended paper pulp into dish pan.

Fold ¼ yd. nylon netting in half and place in a plastic oval embroidery hoop. Cut excess netting from around edges of hoop.

Lay newspaper on work surface and cover with paper towels.

Stir paper pulp in dish pan to help suspend fibers. Take hoop with flush side of screen up and, with a scooping motion, pick up paper pulp. If pulp is not evenly distributed, shake pulp back into water and scoop again. Drain over dish pan.

Place a paper towel over screen and pulp. Gently pat towel to secure towel to pulp. Turn hoop over so flush edge is underneath and place on newspaper. Dab sponge against screen to remove all excess water.

Gently tap hoop and pulp until pulp begins to break away from screen. Pulp will generally come away from middle first, and then, with help, from sides.

Gently remove shape and place on newspaper. Cover with muslin dish towel and firmly roll with rolling pin. Place on aluminum foil to dry. When dry, press with hot iron.

Note: This type of paper is best used with "dry" decorative media, such as pencil, colored pencil, or stamping. It does not tolerate a great deal of moisture because the sizing used to hold the original paper together has been greatly reduced.

hand-tinting photographs

Reproduce a photograph in brown tones at a copy center.

Wipe tips of soft chalk pastels (desired colors for light and shadow flesh tones, cheeks, hair, clothing, and background) using a facial tissue to make certain pastels are clean.

Rub a cotton swab on light facial tone pastel and gently apply to facial area on photo. Blend carefully using a cotton ball. Repeat process using medium facial tone, working in shadow areas and blending edges into light facial tone. Remove any markings outside facial area using a white drafting eraser.

Repeat process for cheeks, hair, clothing, and background. If there is a great deal of detail, soft-leaded colored pencils may be used over pastels.

Color lips using a colored pencil. Work in tiny, light strokes, slowly building up color. Do not draw lips on as doing so will create a hard, unnatural look.

heat-coloring metal

This method uses carefully controlled heat to bring out color in copper. Use a gas range or Bunsen burner. Always hold the copper over the heat with a pair of metal tongs with plastic handles. A little heat will bring out a deep bronze color. Additional heat will bring out shades of purple and aqua. Keep the heat moving and do not overheat an area. Overheating will scorch the metal and all color will be lost. Practice heat-coloring on scraps of copper before beginning project.

marbling paper

Fold several newspapers into strips, 3"-wide x width of shallow tray or cookie pan, for removing paint from surface of water. Lay remaining newspapers on work surface and cover with paper towel.

Mix water and marbling thickener according to manufacturer's instructions. Pour thickened water into tray.

Thin several colors of acrylic paint with water to a runny consistency. Test paint consistency by using a craft stick to touch a drop of paint to surface of water. If paint is too thick, it will sink; if paint is too thin, it will spread too much.

Once paints are to desired consistency, fill eyedropper with one color of paint. Hold dropper close to surface of water and drop paint at regular intervals.

Repeat process using desired number and colors of paint.

Using a stylus or needle, swirl and arrange colors into various designs and patterns.

Hold paper to be marbled at opposite edges and lower to surface of water, touching center of paper first and then edges. Paper must touch surface of water with no air bubbles.

Gently lift paper at one edge and drain over tray. Place paper, pattern side up, on work surface to dry.

Skim paint from water surface with folded strips of newspaper after marbling each sheet of paper. Apply new drops of paint to surface of water and repeat process for desired number of papers.

Place dried marbled paper between two sheets of paper towel and press with a warm iron to flatten.

plastic wrap painting

Cut hot or cold press surface, 90 lb. watercolor paper to desired size.

Paint paper with clear, cool water using 1" sponge paintbrush until surface glistens.

Touch watercolor paint to wet surface of paper using round watercolor paintbrush. Paint some areas dark and some light. Allow paint to diffuse and run.

Place a sheet of plastic wrap over sheet of wet, colored paper. Gently push plastic wrap with fingers until wrinkles and folds of color appear on paper.

Allow paper to thoroughly dry before removing plastic wrap.

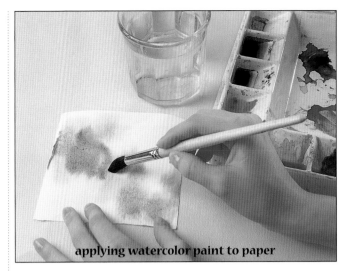
applying watercolor paint to paper

pushing plastic wrap on surface of paper

painting paper with water

removing plastic wrap from dry paper

ribbon embroidery

Before beginning, press ribbon using low heat to remove any creases. Cut ribbon into 18" lengths to reduce the chance of the ribbon fraying while stitching.

scoring

Place a precision ruler onto score marks on cardstock. Slice halfway through cardstock along score marks with a craft knife. Fold at score marks as indicated in project instructions.

sponging paper

Place a quarter-sized pool of 3–4 coordinating colors of acrylic paint on four corners of paper pallette.

Slightly dampen a 1"–2"-wide sea sponge. Dip bottom of sponge into one color of paint and lightly touch to cardstock paper in a random pattern. Cover paper, but allow base color of cardstock to show through. Rotate paper during sponging to vary pattern.

Clean sponge and repeat process using each color of paint.

applying first color of paint to paper

applying second color of paint to paper

tea-dyeing

Bring to a boil, six to eight tea bags in two quarts of water. Turn off heat and steep for at least 20 minutes. Place fabric in tea and soak for at least 30 minutes. The longer fabric is left in tea, the darker the color. Slightly rinse fabric, wring out, and let dry, outside if possible, as fabric tends to darken and spot in sunlight.

transferring

Enlarge pattern as indicated in individual project instructions. Trace pattern to a piece of tracing paper or mylar. Place tracing paper on a light box. Place fabric on top of pattern and trace design onto fabric using a dressmaker's pen

archiving

archival quality

When a scrapbook supplier says their products are archival quality, just what does that mean? It does <u>not</u> mean the products will last forever. There is no way to guarantee a scrapbook will last forever, unless a scrapbook designer intends on chiseling memories in stone. However, archival quality supplies, techniques, and preservation methods are intended to make scrapbooks last for several generations.

There are few binding industry standards when it comes to archival quality products. The term itself is not uniformly used. There is no set number of years a product must last before it can be considered archival quality. Just a label that says archival quality or photo safe is not enough to ensure a product is completely safe. Manufacturers can, and in some cases do, slap the label on any product they sell. Since the term has yet to be uniformly defined, false advertising claims are not an issue.

archival terms

acid: an object that has a pH less than 7.0; an unstable chemical substance that will weaken paper, board, and fabric leading to yellowing and brittleness.

acid free: An object that has a pH of 7.0 or more is said to be free of acid.

acid migration: Even when a product starts out as acid free, there is no guarantee it will stay that way. Acid can move into the product from other high acid objects in close contact, from environmental pollutants, or even from contact with oils in human hands. Acid from high acid products will always migrate to acid free products.

buffering: Calcium carbonate, a colorless or white alkaline chemical is added to buffered products to absorb migrating acids. Buffering adds extra protection, but is still no guarantee against acid. Even buffered products will eventually become acidic if kept in close contact with high acid products for extended periods of time.

chemical stability: Products are said to be chemically stable when their elements are neutral. Chemically stable products do not easily decompose or deteriorate. These products are said to resist changes brought on by contact with natural elements and outside chemicals.

paper terms

acid free paper: products have either had acid removed from the manufacturing process or have been treated to neutralized acids.

lignin free paper: Lignin, the acidic portion of wood pulp, has been removed from the paper making process.

buffered paper: This paper is not only acid free, it is acid absorbent. Buffered paper has added calcium carbonate that will absorb acid that may come into contact with the paper. Many designers will use buffered paper at the front and back of a scrapbook to protect pages from gasses or acids given off by the binder.

acid & lignin free paper: Papers that are both acid free and lignin free are of the highest quality. Products that are only acid free still have lignin in them. Acids in the lignin can build up over time eventually creating problems. These problems may not arise for 20 to 30 years, if at all.

cotton or linen paper: Papers made from wood or wood products can damage photographs if not properly treated. Papers made from cotton or linen are safer, since they do not contain the same acids common in wood products.

permanent paper: A product given this name meets a standard set by a government and paper industry committee. To meet this standard, the product must have a pH level of 7.5 or more, must be free of chemical impurities, must be resistant to tears and folding, and must contain a buffer of calcium carbonate or some other approved alkaline buffer. Permanent paper should also contain cotton or rag fibers.

plastic terms

For maximum protection, archival quality album pages can be enclosed in protective plastic sleeves to prevent damage from dust and handling. Off gassing is the big threat to watch for in plastics. Plastics that are not pH neutral and chemically sound can emit gasses that over time will eat away at the emulsion on photographs, causing colors to fade. Aside from reading labels, the best way to tell a plastic is unsafe is by smelling it. If the plastic has a strong detectable smell, it is probably unsafe for storing photographs.

Several safe plastics are readily available. The following are a few widely used plastics considered safe for direct contact with photographs.

mylar: is the clearest and most expensive way to cover photographs and documents. Mylar is ridged and has a tendency to scratch easily. It is the first choice of professional archivists. This plastic may be purchased in set sheet sizes, in rolls, or in envelopes. Double sided film tape holds the mylar in place around the photograph or document, encasing contents against the elements. Unlike laminating, mylar casing is removable with no damage to the contents.

polypropylene: Like mylar, polypropylene is a clear, translucent plastic. Unlike mylar it is flexible, and scratch resistant. It is also a more economical option. Polypropylene is available most commonly in sheet protectors.

polyethylene: This plastic is very similar to

polypropylene. The difference is that polyethylene has a frosted appearance and is less likely to be affected by static than polypropylene. Polyethylene is also available in sheet protectors.

creating an archival quality scrapbook

Most paper is acidic by nature. If at all possible, keep acidic papers out of scrapbooks. Many craft stores or scrapbook outlets now carry acid free, lignin free paper. Archival quality paper may be slightly more expensive, but the expense is worthwhile. Scrapbooks made with low quality highly acidic papers will fade and tear over time. Low quality paper may even irreversibly damage the very photographs a scrapbook is intended to protect.

Don't use crepe paper or construction paper in a scrap book. These papers will fade and tear quickly, and their colors may bleed onto photographs.

Remember, never place photographs in a "magnetic page" self adhesive photo album. Self stick albums are covered in polyvinyl chloride (PVC), a plastic that releases hydrochloric acid. Acids will actually eat away at pictures, causing them to become yellow and brittle. To make matters worse, the adhesives in these albums will absorb into

photographs over time, making them difficult, if not impossible, to remove. Several companies have tried to reintroduce magnetic page albums using archival quality papers, plastics, and adhesives. Whether or not these products are completely safe is still undetermined.

Items kept in a scrapbook or used to decorate the pages should also be acid free. Scrapbook suppliers sell acid free stickers, cards, photo corners, and pens to compliment acid free background paper and photographs. Permanent pigment pens are the best, since their colors last longer and are less likely to run

or smear over time. Read the label on any pen, or call the manufacturer's customer service line if the label does not indicate the pen is acid free.

A number of materials have been found to be unsafe in direct contact with photographs. Some of these include wood or wood based products, lacquer, or enamels.

Although long term testing hasn't been completed, most scrapbook designers agree that fabric, laces, and ribbons also may be used to embellish scrapbooks. Cotton polyester fabric and notions are recommended and should be washed before use to remove any acids, sizing chemicals, or excess dyes. While the fabric itself may break down over extensive amounts of time, it should not harm photographs. If potential long term fabric problems are still a concern, consider placing buffered paper cutouts between photographs and fabric. Some scrapbook designers have found that brightly colored, poorly made ribbons can occasionally fade or bleed onto photographs. To avoid this, consider placing ribbon around, but not directly on a photograph; or use color copies or duplicates of irreplaceable photographs in questionable designs.

High acid background and embellishing materials are not the only danger to photographs; adhesives used for scrapbooks can also be a source of potential damage. Again, do not use regular transparent tape, high acid rubber cement, super glue, or high acid craft glue in a scrapbook. There are several new acid free adhesives out on the market, some specially designed for scrapbooks. Others, like acid free glue sticks, have been around for some time. Carefully read product labels to make certain adhesives are acid free before using them. If there is a question, call the product customer service line. While they may reveal acid content, many manufacturers will not openly reveal that their product is unsafe.

Truly archival quality scrapbooks should be reversible. This means that photographs placed in the scrapbook can be taken out again with no resulting damage. To make this possible, a scrapbook designer would need to use either a removable adhesive, or photo corners to secure photographs.

removing photographs from self adhesive albums

It may not be too late to save photographs stored in old magnetic page albums. Photographs still in these damaging albums should be removed immediately. If photographs don't come up easily, they may have already begun bonding with the adhesive. Try using a thin cake spatula to pry up old photographs. If they still stick, use a warm blow dryer to melt the gum between the picture and the page. Running waxed dental floss between the photograph and the adhesive page can also help to remove photographs. If, even after effort, photographs still won't come free, get color copies of them to add to an archival quality scrapbook.

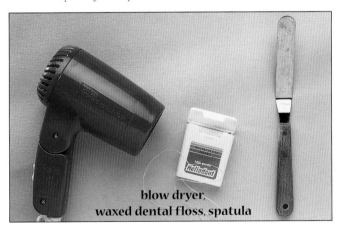

blow dryer, waxed dental floss, spatula

saving non-archival quality memorabilia

Some scrapbook designers may want to include high acid papers in their scrapbooks such as newspaper clippings, children's artwork, school report cards, or event tickets. All of these paper mementos can be a source of high acid content. Newspaper, one of the highest in acid content, is made with a low grade paper which will become yellow and brittle within only a few years. Photographs and papers that come into contact with high acid paper may absorb some of the acids. Newspaper inks are unstable, high in acid, and may bleed onto surrounding photographs or papers.

There are a number of *safe* ways to include these high acid memories in albums. High acid items can be photocopied onto acid free paper. Original documents may be placed in clear mylar envelopes where they can be viewed without acid escaping. Documents can also be sprayed with a neutralizer. The spray coats the paper and neutralizes acid levels. Display the sprayed document on buffered paper. The buffered paper will absorb acid as the levels rise over time. Buffered paper should be changed every few years to keep it's absorbency effective.

finding acid-free scrapbook supplies

Scrapbook suppliers are a great source for papers, stickers, pens, and other acid-free products. Standard craft stores are starting to carry the items too. If a product is not labeled acid free, a pH testing pen may be used to test for acid content. These pH pens can also be used to check for acid content in documents, certificates, or other paper mementos a scrapbook designer may consider including in page design. *See* **pH Testing Pen** *on page 10.*

creating albums just for fun

Often, scrapbook designers may decide to create short term scrapbooks just for the fun of it. These albums are intended to be used now, without the extra care needed to make photographs last for future generations. There is nothing wrong with breaking all the rules and putting together a quick, fun album. When creating this type of scrapbook, consider using color copies of irreplaceable photographs or duplicates of photographs instead of running the risk of sacrificing one-of-a-kind priceless pictures. Duplicates or color copies of photographs may also be used when the acid content of fun designs may cause long term damage to photographs. So go ahead and use wood, bright fabrics or ribbons, water based pens, newspaper clippings, and high acid papers. Just think twice before using photographs that can not be replaced.

alternatives to traditional scrapbooks

Scrapbooks are not the only safe way to store memories. While a standard shoe box is not safe, an archival photography storage box can be a great place to tuck away mementos. Photographs and clippings can also be arranged in a simple collage and displayed on a wall. A collage of items from a vacation can include more than just photographs. Local currency, event tickets, maps, post cards, stamps, local magazine or newspaper clippings, travel brochures, and more can be included to preserve memories of time away from home. If the collage is only intended for short term display, extensive archival precautions may not be necessary. If the collage is intended to hang for several years, consider testing papers and other mementos for acid content before including them, or using color copies or duplicates of irreplaceable photographs. *See **Scrapbook Alternatives** on pages 120–127 for more ideas.*

alternatives to plastic page protectors

Photographs should not be allowed to rub up against each other in a scrapbook. Plastic page protectors are only one way to keep photographs on adjacent pages from touching. Many of the designs in this book are interactive, providing scrapbook browsers an opportunity to open pop-out features, or slide out designs. These features would be inaccessible trapped in a plastic covered page. Fortunately, there are other options for page protection. Many scrapbooks have built in tissue paper dividers used to separate pages from each other. If a scrapbook does not have dividers and plastic page protectors are not an alternative, consider placing photographs on every other page to keep designs from rubbing against each other.

storing negatives

Many people consider the printed picture the most important part of the photography experience to preserve. Negatives, though frequently ignored, are just as important as the photographs themselves. With preserved negatives, unlimited new photographs can be obtained at a minimal price. If only the photograph is saved, reproduction or restoration prices are more expensive.

Negatives should be organized and stored with just as much thought and care as prints. Negatives are not always safely stored in the envelopes sent from the photo lab. Negatives should not be stored touching each other, since rubbing can damage negatives. The best way to store negatives is in archival quality plastic sleeves. These clear divided sheets allow negatives to be organized and viewed while protecting them from the elements. The sleeves can then be organized into 3-ring binders. Negative storage sleeves can be purchased from a photography supply store.

Negative Storage Sleeves

Photographs can be reproduced from well-preserved black and white negatives almost indefinitely. Color negatives, no matter how carefully stored have a shorter life. The color dyes in negatives will begin to shift over time. Within 15 or 20 years, the color negative will no longer produce a first rate image. While colors may not be true, an image will still be present. Professional photo labs can correct some of the color problems in old negatives.

safe scrapbook storage

Most people unknowingly store their scrapbooks in the worst possible places. Attics and basements are never the place to store photographs. Photographs don't stand up well under extremes of heat, cold, or humidity. Commercial storage sheds are also an unwise place to store photographs. Even though some storage units are climate controlled, potential water damage or theft can not be completely ruled out.

The best place to keep scrapbooks is in the part of the house the family lives in. Since heat and cold are controlled for human comfort in living areas, scrapbooks will stay within safe limits. Another option, is to keep archival scrapbooks, photographs or negatives in a bank safe deposit box. Most bank boxes are kept secure and many are even climate controlled to keep humidity and temperature levels constant.

It is always a good idea to keep duplicates of favorite photographs somewhere besides home. In the event of a fire, flood, or other natural disaster, at least some photographs will survive. Duplicates can be kept with family, friends, or in a bank deposit box.

Light can also be damaging to scrapbooks. Just as direct sunlight will eventually fade carpet and furniture, it will fade scrapbooks and pictures. Although scrapbooks can be safely displayed on a coffee table or bookcase, they are safest in archival quality storage boxes. Boxes keep out light and dust. If scrapbooks are displayed in the open, make certain they are kept out of direct sunlight.

storing photographs on CD-ROM

The safest and most compact way to store photographs is on CD-ROM's. Photographs scanned in a high resolution format into a computer and stored on a computer compact disc will last throughout the years without fading, tearing, or deteriorating. Best of all, home storage space is saved since just one small compact disc will hold hundreds of photographs. In addition, short sound or video clips can be added to CD-ROM's to compliment photographs.

While CD-ROM manufacturers frequently claim this medium lasts forever, many industry analysts disagree. A number of studies conclude the lifetime of a compact disc is only about 75 to 100 years.

To store photographs on CD-ROM at home, a computer, color scanner, and compact disc writer or burner are necessary. While many homes have computers, few families own scanners or burners. Lower resolution photographs can also be scanned and stored on a removable storage disk. The removable disks are less expensive, but the life of the stored photographs may not be as long as for those stored on CD-ROM.

Removable Storage Disks   **CD-ROM**

If purchasing expensive computer hardware is not an option, photographs can be taken to computer graphic imaging centers for scanning and storage. Look in the yellow pages for a local graphics center that offers the scanning service.

Some graphics centers will allow customers to lay out their photographs in a page layout similar to a standard scrapbook, allowing space for further embellishment and text. Many centers even provide indexing utilities to assist customers in organizing and finding photographs on the compact discs.

Most photographic developing services provide less elaborate scanning and compact disc duplication services. Just about anywhere photographs are dropped off for developing, CD-ROM scanning and duplication service is available. Customers can have almost anything transferred onto compact disc: unprocessed film, negatives, slides, or color or black & white photographs. Prices vary by store, but usually run around $1 per scan, which, in this case, includes the price of the compact disk. Services can usually store at least one hundred high resolution scans on a compact disk. Some, with more advanced systems, may be able to store more.

Although many scanning services provide mail order services, most say customers should never mail irreplaceable photographs. Send color copies of one-of-a-kind photographs in for placement on compact disc.

family history

researching family history

Scrapbooks are more than a way of preserving the present for the future, they are a way of discovering the past. As scrapbook designers prepare pages to preserve memories of their current family, they may also want to consider researching their family origins.

start at home

The best place to start a search for origins is at home. Look around the house for items of genealogical value. These include:

Birth certificates
Family bibles
High school or college diplomas
Marriage announcements or invitations
Marriage certificates
Military discharge papers
Needlework samplers
Obituaries
Old initialed flatware
Old passports
Old quilts (often signed by their maker)
Photographs

Look through the items for clues from the past to find the answers to the commonly asked questions, who, what, where, when, how, and why.

Again, when home resources run out, try checking with extended family members. Contact older living relatives. They may have more items of genealogical value, or may remember family stories that can be of help in the search for past generations.

assembling clues from the past

A pedigree chart is the best way to compile genealogical information. The chart resembles the branches of a tree and has room for names and the dates and places of birth, marriage, and death of each individual in a family.

The first name on the list should be the person who the research is done for. Branching out from that person is their mother and father. Branching out from both mother and father are grandparents and then great-grandparents on each side.

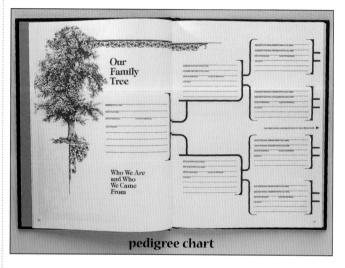

pedigree chart

With each progressive generation back, ancestors multiply. Many researchers choose to go back four or five generations. Many Americans choose to research back far enough to identify their family's first immigrants.

Do not make the mistake many researchers make in only researching the surname line. A person is just as closely related to ancestors who bare different surnames as to those who bare the same last name. Leaving a mother's, grandmother's, or great-grandmother's line unexplored, leaves the research process unfinished.

To begin, try putting together a four- or five-generation pedigree chart. Fill in the chart as much as possible. Make certain to use complete names when known. Dates and places for birth, death, and marriage can be estimated if they are not known.

filling in the gaps

After all known information about a family has been recorded in the pedigree, the real detective work can begin. Look for gaps and holes in the assembled information to find out where to begin the search.

To fill in the gaps, go from the known to the unknown. Knowing the name of a grandfather, can lead to the names of his father and mother. His parents' names may be found on his birth certificate or marriage certificate. Once his parents' names are found, their parents can be found in the same way. By digging through public records, the search can begin to turn up the names, dates, and places necessary to complete the family pedigree.

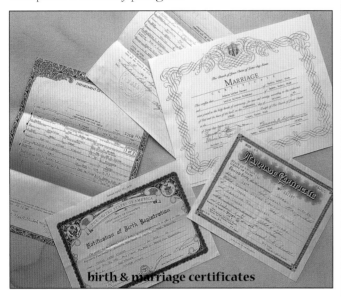
birth & marriage certificates

where to find records
—local records

Birth certificates, death certificates, and marriage certificates are typically kept in town or county courthouses. If accessing them in person is impossible, requests can also be made by mail. Many requests can not be met since town or county records departments do not always have the time or the employees to spare looking up information. It is always a good idea to include an offer for payment for research services and a self-addressed stamped envelope with any request. Many courthouses have set prices for records searches. A quick phone call, to obtain specific procedures, is a good idea. Include in any request for a records search the complete name of the individual and important dates that may identify the record.

Other official records kept on a county level can be

of help to the researcher. Probate records provide a wealth of information. The most important variety is the last will and testament. Wills typically list the names of children and spouses. In some cases wills may be the only time the first name of a wife will be mentioned.

—state records

Many states keep duplicate birth, death, or marriage records at the state level. Each state has an address researchers can write to to ask for records searches. The Department of Health and Human Services produces a booklet called, "Where to Write for Vital Records–Births, Deaths, Marriages, and Divorces". An up-to-date copy of the booklet can be obtained by sending a self addressed envelope and $2.25 to:

Superintendent of Documents
Government Printing Office
Washington, D.C. 20402-9325

The information is also available free of charge on the internet at the following address:

http://www.cdc.gov/nchsww/nchshome.htm

If the state does not have the records requested, they will usually forward the request to the local office that does. Most states have specific fees for document searches. Fees are listed in the Department of Health's booklet.

—federal records

Federal records of use to the researcher include: census records, military pension records, passenger arrival lists, and naturalization records. Census records can be obtained for a fee by writing to the following address:

U.S. Department of Commerce
Bureau of the Census
Pittsburgh, Kansas 66762

Military pension records and passenger arrival lists are kept in the National Archives. Although a personal visit to the archives is encouraged by many professional genealogists, records can be requested by mail by writing:

National Archives and Records Service
NNC
Washington, D.C. 20408

When requesting information, provide as much information as possible. Including full names, dates, and, places.

—other sources

Government documents are not the only source of information for researching family history. A researcher can also turn to newspaper archives, internet web sites, records of private organizations and societies, school records, church records, and even cemetery grave markers.

Most newspapers print birth, marriage, and death announcements. If a researcher has good idea of when an event occurred, they may be able to find the announcement of it in local newspaper archives. Marriage announcements and obituaries contain valuable genealogical information. Together, the two announcements usually contain birth, marriage, and death dates; names of parents and children; places of residence; occupation; schools attended; and organization membership information. Although many newspapers have been microfilmed and indexed, many have not. Phone calls to the papers covering the locality where an ancestor married or died can tell a researcher whether or not the obituaries and marriage announcements have been archived.

The world wide web via the internet is a vast and valuable resource when searching for family members. With a computer, a modem, and an internet service provider, information that would have taken an extended amount of time to receive by more traditional means can now be acquired in minutes. Once logged on to the internet, access a search engine and use keywords (special words or phrases that go instantly from one location, or site, to another over the web) that relate to this topic such as "geneology," "family origin," or "birth and death record." If a home computer setup as described above is not an option, look to the local library. Many libraries now have up-to-date computers that are designated for patrons' use in performing internet research.

Records of private organizations, clubs, and societies may turn up some clues worth looking for. Much of the information stored by organizations may be as simple as the member's name and date of joining, but occasionally records also include names of the member's parents, wife, or children. Some membership records include detailed information on a member's age, educational background, occupation, religion, and occasionally even a photograph.

College and university records can also be a source of information. Rosters, rolls, yearbooks, and enrollment records kept by many colleges and universities may include information about a student's residence and may include the names of parents.

Churches kept records of births, marriages, and deaths before the government ever began documenting vital statistics. To obtain information from existing churches, first contact the ecclesiastical leader of the local church. Even if church leaders don't have the records, they may know where records are stored. For churches no longer in existence, contact the local historical society, to find out where the old records are kept.

Many churches offer family history services to the public. The Church of Jesus Christ of Latter Day Saints (the Mormons) has one of the largest family history services in the world. Since they consider genealogy a moral imperative, the LDS church has sent microfilm crews throughout the world to duplicate documents. The family history library, located near the church's headquarters in Salt Lake City, Utah, contains millions of microfilmed documents. These documents are available to the public and copies can be requested through any local LDS church branch throughout the world. Many researchers have found an afternoon spent in the family history library can save years of research.

Local historical societies can be a source of genealogical help and advice. Check with a local society, or call or write to the society near the ancestor being searched for.

Cemetery gravemarkers can be a help to the

researcher. In the past when people more frequently stayed in the same place for generations, entire families were often buried together. Many early graves were even dug on a family's own land. A pilgrimage to a family grave site can sometimes help turn up potential clues. Complete names are often recorded on gravemarkers when they were never written down on other documents. A woman who was listed only as Mrs. John Smith in documents will sometimes have her given name and maiden name on a marker.

laws associated with records

The Right to Privacy Act of 1974, makes some recent records inaccessible. Frequently, even though the records are not available to the public, they will be made open to genealogical researchers who are themselves listed in the records.

Many states have their own laws governing the release of records. Some will only release records to the public which were created 75 to 100 years ago. Since most information about the last 75 to 100 years can be found in home sources, record holds do not bar many genealogists from learning about their ancestors.

Laws sealing adoption records are much harder to research past. In old birth records, information about the biological parents of a child or the child's legitimacy was openly recorded in public documents. Modern adoption records are typically sealed by courts, unable to be opened without a court order rescinding the sealing.

displaying family histories

Once a family pedigree chart has been completed, it makes a perfect addition to a family scrapbook. Even a partially complete chart is of value to future generations.

photography

improving photographs

Great scrapbooks start with great photographs. Although professional photographs are wonderful additions to a scrapbook, using a professional photographer for all photographs is not practical, or necessary. With a few tips, even inexperienced photographers can improve the quality of their snapshots.

camera viewfinders

The viewfinder on a camera is not a window through the lens. Often lens obstructions will not be visible though the viewfinder. It is up to the photographer to make certain lens obstructions are removed. Before taking a photograph, make certain the lens cap is removed, the camera strap is clear, and no fingers cover the lens. Periodically, check to see if the lens needs cleaning. A dirty lens will only show in the photographs, not the viewfinder.

correct image cropping

What is seen in the viewfinder is not always what shows up in a photograph. Black or faint yellow lines in a viewfinder show where the image is cropped. Even though the area around the lined off rectangle is visible, it will not get into the picture. Avoid mistakes, such as cropping off people's heads, by keeping the desired image within the lines.

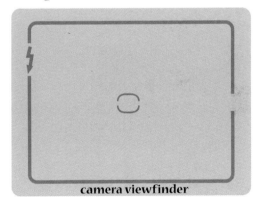

camera viewfinder

camera angles

Variety can be added to photographs by changing the angles at which photographs are taken. Try looking through the camera viewfinder at the subject from low, high, and normal camera angles to see which will look best. Children's photographs are often better if the photographer kneels down to the child's level before taking the shot. Many older people find photographs taken from a slightly higher angle more appealing.

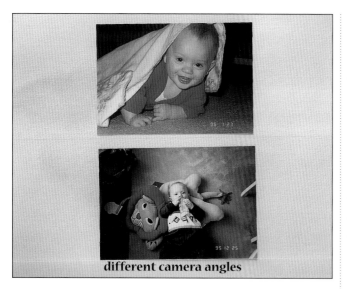

different camera angles

outdoor photographs

Direct sunlight is too strong for taking photographs. Direct sunlight can cause harsh shadows on a squinting subject's face. In the past, film was not sensitive enough to take photographs without sun in the subject's face. Today's film is sensitive enough to work without the harsh lighting.

The best lighting for outdoor photographs comes at sunrise and sunset. When taking photographs during other times of day, try taking the shots in the shade or under cloud cover. Light harshness can also be cut down when the photographer faces the sun, using the subject to create shade for the photograph. When using this method, the sun acts as a backlight on the subject. If at all possible, try to avoid taking photographs at noon. At noon, the sun comes straight down on subjects creating dark shadows on their faces.

shadows & under cloud cover

causes of red eye

The flash from the camera travels into the subject's eyes and reflects at almost a straight angle back to the camera lens. This reflects the blood vessels in the eye, making the eye appear red.

preventing red eye

Red eye is most common in cameras where the lens is too close to the flash. When selecting a camera, try to choose a model with the lens as far away from the flash as possible. The wider the angle of reflection, the less likely red eye will occur. Some cameras also have a red eye reduction feature. The red eye reducing cameras emit a small flash before the main photo flash. The two flashes meet, counteracting the red eye reflection. Some photographers have found that placing a light behind the photographer may also help to cut down on the problem.

correcting red eye

Fixing red eyes on photographs is possible using special red eye pens. The pens contain a dye that filters out the color red, allowing natural eye features to show through. Pen dye should be applied only to the red area on the eye. If applied to the white of the eye, the pen dye will cause the white to appear blue.

film tips

A film's sensitivity to light is rated by its speed. The higher the film speed, the more sensitive it is to light. A lower film speed needs more light. A higher film speed needs less light. While a multi-purpose film speed might meet most photography needs, a photographer may want to purchase additional rolls of film for special lighting situations. Film should be used promptly and developed quickly. Use negative film for prints and slide film for slides. Don't allow film to be exposed to x-rays. Ask to have film hand checked at airports and don't ever put film in luggage where x-ray inspections are strongest. Don't expose film to heat. Never leave exposed or unexposed film in a hot car or in direct sunlight.

photo labs

Good photographs come from good photo labs. Avoid the temptation to save money by going with a lower quality lab. Incorrect developing can mean the difference between a photograph that lasts and a photograph that quickly fades.

black & white vs. color

Black & white photographs last a great deal longer than color photographs. As the years pass, the dyes that create the color in photographs shift, causing images to fade and blur. Often fading occurs so gradually, it is almost unnoticeable. When there is no perfect original to compare a faded photograph with, color fading can be virtually undetectable. Color photography can still have a place in an archival quality album. Black & white photographs should be taken periodically to add to a family photographic record, but they do not need to replace color photography. Many scrapbook designers recommend taking a set of black & white photographs every six months to one year to preserve family history, in the event color photographs deteriorate.

photographic restoration

Photographic restoration has come a long way in the last few years. It is now possible to effectively restore damaged photographs at an affordable price. In the past, damaged photographs could only be restored by hand using pencils, dyes, chalks, and oils. Work was typically done directly on the damaged photo. The process was time consuming and expensive. Traditional methods can still be used today, but a good photographic artist will charge $25 to $40 an hour on average.

The most popular new method for restoration is digital. The damaged photograph is scanned into a computer where the digital copy can be manipulated by a photographic artist. Using this method, restoration experts can mend torn photos, add backgrounds, remove staining, enhance images, correct colors, and fix water damage discoloration. Artists can even make cosmetic changes to photographs, like removing teen's braces or blemishes.

While the digital restoration process is still time consuming, it is much more efficient compared to traditional methods. Plus, a computer artist can always undo a change that doesn't work. A traditional artist has to start over if there is a mistake. Often when work is done on the photograph itself, mistakes can cause further damage to the photograph. Once a photograph has been restored, copies can be made from it.

Digital restoration prices can vary based on the complexity of the work being done. Typically prices begin at around $25 and can reach up into hundreds of dollars depending on the complexity of work requested.

Digital restoration does not repair the damaged photograph itself. It creates a new undamaged print that looks just like the old photograph. To restore or preserve the damaged photograph itself, a photographic conservator is needed. Conservators clean the original portrait, mend it, and, in some cases, can even intensify the original image. If possible, get a second opinion before turning a photograph over to a conservator for work. Many of the cleaning processes used in photographic conservation can cause more damage than good. Never give a cherished photograph to an inexperienced conservator. More damage to photographs can be caused by good intentions than by neglect.

before & after photographic restoration

29

Interactive Pop-up Pictures

picture pop-up

materials

Album: expandable spine

Cardboard: lightweight

Cording: coordinating

Double-sided fusible web

Fabric: coordinating cotton print; coordinating cotton
solid; white cotton; assorted coordinating scraps (8)

Photo transfer paper

Quilt batting: lightweight

general supplies & tools

Glue gun and glue sticks
Iron/ironing board
Marker: disappearing fabric
Measuring tape
Scissors: fabric; pinking shears

instructions

1. Measure album cover. Add 2" to height and width measurements and cut two pieces from cotton print fabric for front and back album covers.

2. Center and lay front cover on right side of one fabric piece and mark placement using disappearing fabric marker.

3. Enlarge **Seasons Patterns** at right and on page 32 to desired size for album cover. Refer to General Instructions for **Fusible Appliqué** on page 15. Trace outer patterns onto paper side of fusible web. Iron fusible web to back side of white fabric following manufacturer's instructions.

4. Copy photographs onto photo transfer paper at a copy center, following manufacturer's instructions. Reduce or enlarge as necessary to fit traced patterns.

5. Position photo transfers over traced patterns and iron onto white fabric. Cut out patterns, trimming them ⅛". Remove paper backing and iron onto front cover fabric piece.

6. Cut quilt batting to fit front and back covers. Hot-glue batting to top side of front and back covers.

7. Lay front and back fabric pieces face down. Center and lay covers on top of fabric, batting side down. Mark spine holes. Wrap and hot-glue fabric edges to inside of covers.

8. Cut cardboard into two pieces, ⅛" smaller than inside covers. Cut cotton fabric into two pieces, 1" larger than cardboard pieces. Lay cardboard onto fabric. Wrap and hot-glue fabric edges to inside of cardboard. Hot-glue fabric-covered cardboard to inside front and back covers to hide all raw edges. Cut out spine holes. Hot-glue cording around edges of front and back covers.

9. Trace seasonal motifs onto paper side of fusible web. Cut around patterns. Iron motifs to back sides of fabric scraps and cut out.

10. Remove paper backing and iron patterns as shown in photograph onto solid cotton fabric. Cut out motifs using pinking shears and leaving a ⅛"-wide border. Lay appliquéd motifs over photo transfers and hot-glue top edge of motifs to cover. Lift motifs to reveal photographs underneath.

11. Reassemble album.

Seasons Patterns

Seasons Patterns (cont.)

Verse:

God made a world out of his dreams,
Of magic mountains, oceans, and streams.
Prairies and plains and wooded land,
Then paused and said, "I need someone to
    stand . . .
On top of the mountains, to conquer the seas
Explore the plains and climb the trees.
Someone to start out small and grow
Sturdy, strong, like a tree" and so . . .
He created boys, full of spirit and fun. . . .

— Author Unknown

Picture Pop-up

baby bundle

materials

Cardstock: coordinating colors (3)
Decorative paper: baby theme
Die-cut shape: diaper pin
Stickers: ⅜" alphabet

general supplies & tools

Adhesive
Craft knife
Marker: fine point black
Ruler: metal-edge
Scissors: craft; decorative edge

instructions

1. Cut decorative paper to fit album page using craft scissors. Adhere paper to album page.

2. Enlarge **Envelope & Heart Patterns** at right and trace onto different colors of cardstock. Cut out shapes. Slit mark on envelope with a craft knife

3. Refer to general instructions for **Scoring** on page 18. Score and fold envelope as shown on pattern.

4. Adhere heart to top flap of envelope as shown on photograph on opposite page.

5. Cut out a ⅛" section from one side of die-cut pin. Adhere pin to heart. Draw slits on heart with black marker so pin appears pinned to heart.

6. Cut photograph to fit inside of envelope using decorative edge scissors. Use alphabet stickers for child's name and birth date and attach to inside envelope flaps.

7. Use alphabet stickers for desired message and attach to second cardstock paper. Cut around message using decorative edge scissors. Adhere message to third cardstock paper. Cut paper. Adhere message and envelope to album page.

Envelope & Heart Patterns

score and fold

cut slit

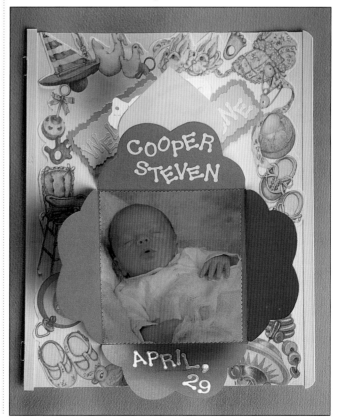

Baby Bundle

33

happy birthday

materials
Cardstock: coordinating (6)
Embossing powder: clear
Pigment ink pad: coordinating bright variegated
Sponges, 3-D self stick: ⅛ diameter x ¼ thick (3)
Stamp: birthday theme
Stickers: birthday theme

general supplies & tools
Adhesive
Craft knife
Heat tool
Ruler: metal edge
Scissors: craft; decorative edge (2)

instructions
1. Cut one sheet of cardstock to fit album page using decorative edge scissors. Adhere paper to album page.

2. Cut ⅛ off all sides of second sheet of cardstock using second pair of decorative edge scissors. Fold paper in half to form card.

3. Open card. Measure and mark 2" in from each side of card at center fold. Make two vertical slits at marks, extending 1" above and below center fold, using a craft knife and ruler. Refer to General Instructions for **Scoring** on page 18. Score between ends of slits using a craft knife and ruler as shown in **Diagram 1** on opposite page. Slowly fold card so slit section pops up.

4. Cut ⅛ from sides and 1¼ from top and bottom edges of a third sheet of cardstock using second pair of decorative edge scissors. Fold paper in half and adhere over top of folded card, making certain not to adhere center section where pop-up is located.

5. Enlarge **Cake, Candle, & Balloon Patterns** on opposite page. Trace onto desired colors of cardstock. Use one balloon to trace onto photograph. Cut out shapes and photograph using craft scissors.

6. Adhere cake layers together. Adhere frosting over top of each layer. Adhere flames to candles and adhere candles to cake. Adhere decorated cake to front of pop up section.

7. Stamp a balloon using birthday theme stamp and pigment ink pad. Apply embossing powder over stamped design following manufacturer's instructions. Heat and cool.

8. Attach balloons above cake to inside of card using 3-D sponges and adhere.

9. Use stickers to embellish inside and outside of card and album page as desired.

Circles can be used to make balloons. Just draw in the string and add a stem. Highlight the curve of the balloon with a scrap of white paper.

Cake, Candle, & Balloon Patterns

Make a pop-up gumball machine. Cut out circles of all sizes and colors to look like gumballs and some to look like coins. Cut photographs into circles, too. Include the childhood verse, "Bubblegum, bubblegum, in a dish. How many pieces do you wish?"

Diagram 1

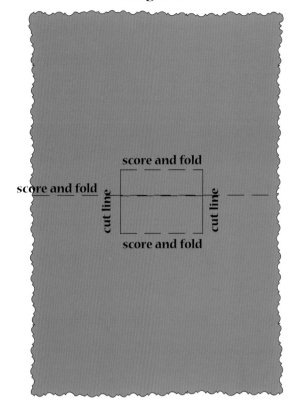

score and fold

score and fold

cut line

cut line

score and fold

Happy Birthday

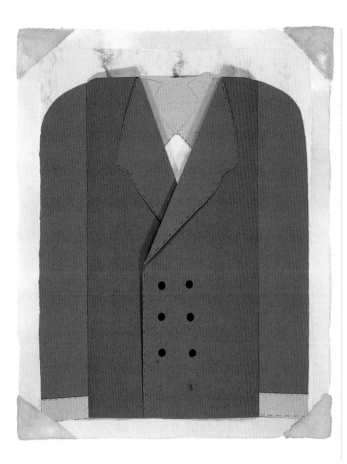

daddy's coat

materials

Cardstock: coordinating (4)
Decorative paper: coordinating (2)
Medium-weight paper: coordinating

general supplies & tools

Adhesive
Craft knife
Paper punch: round
Pen: point .03 black
Ruler: metal edge
Scissors: craft; decorative edge

instructions

1. Cut one sheet of decorative paper to fit album page using craft scissors. Adhere paper to album page.

2. Enlarge **Daddy's Coat Patterns** below and trace onto cardstock. Trace tie onto second sheet of decorative paper. Cut out shapes.

Daddy's Coat Patterns

— — **score and fold**
· — · — · **placement lines**

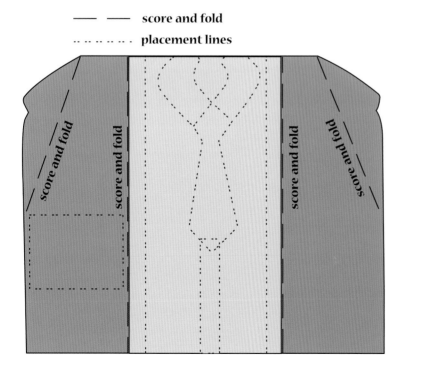
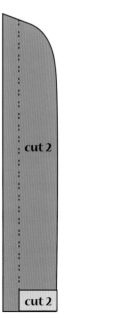
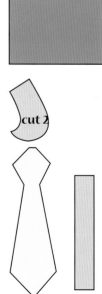

3. Refer to General Instructions for **Scoring** on page 18. Score and fold coat as shown on pattern.

4. Refer to photgraph on opposite page. Adhere cuffs to sleeves. Adhere sleeves to back of coat. Adhere pocket to left inside flap of coat. Adhere shirt to inside of coat. Adhere collar, placket, and tie to shirt. Adhere assembled coat to album page.

5. Draw buttons on placket, and draw stitching lines around cuffs, lapels, pocket, collar, and placket using black pen. Write desired message on right inside flap of coat.

6. Punch six "buttons" from cardstock using round paper hole punch. Adhere buttons to front right flap of coat.

7. Cut a 7" x 2½" strip from medium-weight paper. Fold strip into three 2¼" squares. Fold remaining ¼" under. Cut photos slightly smaller than each folded square using decorative edge scissors. Adhere photos to folded squares. Adhere ¼" fold to inside of pocket.

Daddy's Coat

sunflower pocket

materials
Cardstock: coordinating
Stickers: ¾" alphabet; decorative

general supplies & tools
Adhesive
Craft knife
Markers: extra fine point; medium point
Ruler: metal edge
Scissors: decorative edge

instructions
1. Refer to General Instructions for **Scoring** on page 18. Score and fold sides and bottom of cardstock paper, ¾" from edges, as shown on **Diagram 1** on page 38, using a craft knife and ruler. Cut 4½" off top of paper using decorative edge scissors.

2. Adhere folded edges of paper to album page, creating a pocket. Use alphabet and decorative stickers to embellish pocket as desired. Draw decorative lines between stickers with markers.

Diagram 1

halloween

materials
Cardstock: coordinating (3)
Stickers: Halloween theme

general supplies & tools
Adhesive
Pen: point .03 black
Scissors: craft

instructions
1. Cut a sheet of cardstock to fit album page. Adhere paper to album page.

2. Enlarge **Tombstone Pattern** on opposite page and trace onto cardstock, using different colors for fronts and backs of tombstones. Trace tombstones onto photographs. Cut out all.

3. Cut three 1" x ⅛" strips from cardstock. Fold strips in half and adhere to back of tombstones and album page for hinges. Align photographs with tombstones and adhere to album page.

4. Use pen to write epitaphs on tombstones and stickers to embellish album page as desired.

Tombstone Pattern

cut 3

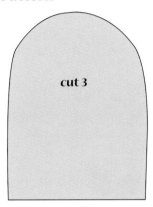
cut 3

Halloween

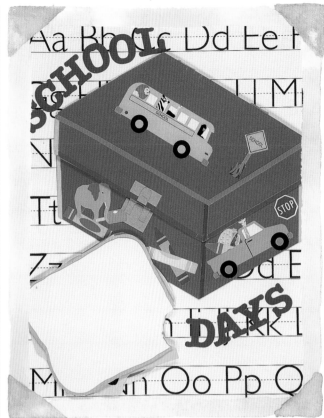

school lunch

materials
Cardstock: "food" colors (9); trunk colors (3)
Decorative paper: coordinating (2)
Stickers: ¼" alphabet; decorative; stripes

general supplies & tools
Adhesive
Marker: fine point black
Scissors: craft; decorative edge

instructions
1. Cut one sheet of decorative paper to fit album page using craft scissors. Adhere paper to album page.

2. Enlarge **Food Patterns** and **Lunch Box Patterns** on page 40 and trace onto cardstock, using different colors for inside and outside of lunch box. Cut out.

3. Refer to photograph above. Adhere inside lunch box and inside lid shapes to inside of lunch box. Cut two

39

⅛" x 2" strips from cardstock. Fold strips in half and adhere to inside of box and lid for hinges. Adhere latch to lunch box.

4. Cut a 3" square from second sheet of decorative paper for napkin. Fold as shown in **Diagram 1** and adhere to inside of lunch box.

5. Adhere leaf and stem to apple. Write teacher's class and year on apple using black marker. Adhere chocolate chips to cookie. Adhere apple and cookie to inside of lunch box.

6. Cut class photo to fit inside lid of lunch box using decorative edge scissors.

7. Adhere bread to crusts. Cut two ⅛" x 2" strips from cardstock. Fold strips in half and adhere to inside of bread for hinges.

8. Cut two ¼" x 1" strips. Fold strips in half and adhere to cheese and lettuce, and to lettuce and meat for hinges.

9. Adhere individual photographs to cheese, lettuce and meat. Adhere meat to inside bottom slice of bread. Close sandwich and adhere to album page.

10. Use alphabet, decorative, and stripe stickers to embellish album page and lunch box as desired.

Food Patterns

cut 2

cut 3

cut 7

Diagram 1

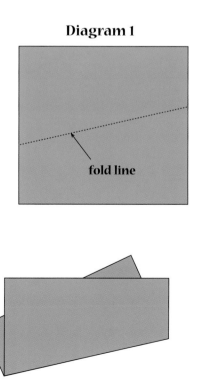

fold line

Lunchbox Patterns

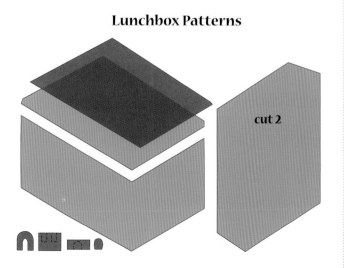

cut 2

40

School Lunch

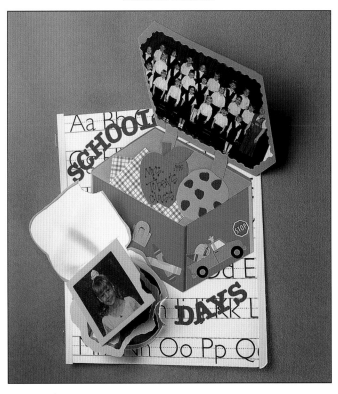

holiday stocking

materials
Cardstock: coordinating (6)
Decorative paper: coordinating (2)
Grosgrain ribbon: ⅛"-wide coordinating
Stickers: Christmas theme

general supplies & tools
Adhesive
Craft knife
Marker: fine point
Scissors: craft; decorative edge

instructions
1. Cut one sheet of decorative paper to fit album page using craft scissors. Adhere paper to album page.

2. Enlarge **Holiday Stocking Patterns** on page 42 and trace stocking, cuff, "Ho," tree, crayon, gingerbread boy, and train patterns onto cardstock, using different colors for trains. Cut out shapes, cutting one train slightly smaller than other. Slit designated mark on cuff using a craft knife.

3. Trace heel pattern onto second sheet of decorative paper and cut out. Adhere heel to stocking.

4. Adhere edges of stocking and cuff to album page. Do not adhere centers or top edge of stocking.

5. Cut three 2" squares from cardstock using decorative edge scissors. Adhere squares to album page. Adhere "Ho" to squares.

6. Trace gingerbread boy, crayon, and tree shapes onto photos. Cut out photos, slightly within cutting line, using craft scissors. Adhere photos to cardstock shapes.

7. Adhere train shapes together. Write "Christmas" and year on train using marker.

8. Cut ribbon into four equal lengths. Adhere one end of each ribbon to back of shapes. Place opposite ribbon end through slit on stocking cuff and adhere in place. Gently stuff stocking with shapes.

9. Attach stickers to form garland across bottom of stocking cuff.

Holiday Stocking Patterns

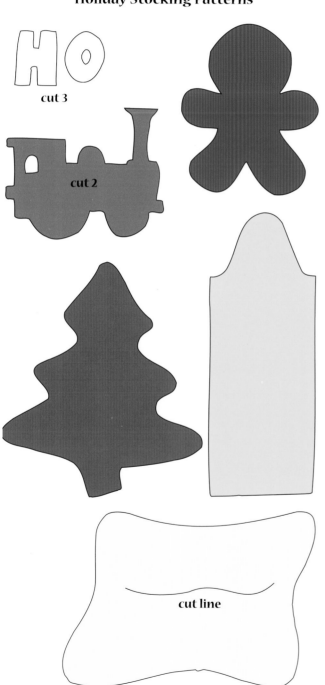

cut 3

cut 2

cut line

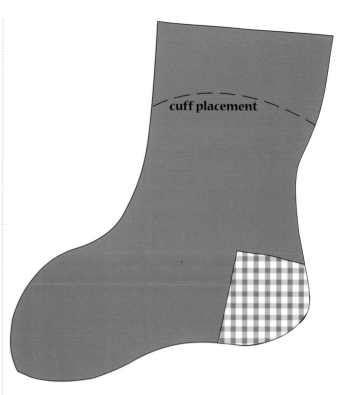

cuff placement

Holiday Stocking

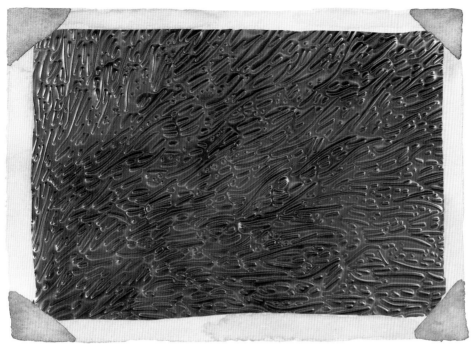

fold-out pets

Passion for Pets

materials
Cardboard: heavy
Copper tooling foil: 36 gauge
Decorative paper: coordinating
Handmade papers: coordinating

general supplies & tools
Adhesive
Embossing tool
Glue gun and glue sticks
Newspapers: small stack
Scissors: craft; old or tin snips

instructions
1. Cut two pieces of cardboard to desired size of album cover using craft scissors.

2. Refer to General Instructions for **Cutting Metal** on page 14. Cut copper foil ⅛" larger than cardboard using old craft scissors.

3. Refer to General Instructions for

Tradition   See page 46

Embossing Copper on page 14. Lay copper on newspapers. Press desired pattern onto copper using embossing tool.

4. Refer to General Instructions for **Heat-Coloring Metal** on page 16. Color embossed copper pieces as desired. Hot-glue copper to cardboard, folding and wrapping excess copper to back of cardboard as shown in **Diagram 1**, to form front and back album covers. Snip corners, if needed.

5. Cut handmade and decorative papers slightly smaller than album cover using craft scissors. Overlap decorative papers ¼" and adhere together to create a continuous page, to desired length. Gently tear handmade papers into a variety of widths. Mix papers and adhere to back of decorative paper page.

6. Fold one end of handmade paper side of page under ¼" and adhere, decorative paper side down, to inside of front album cover. Gently fold page, accordion-style, to create album pages. Fold end of last page under ¼" and adhere, decorative paper-side down, to inside of back album cover. If necessary, adhere additional decorative and handmade papers together for even distribution of pages.

Diagram 1

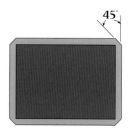
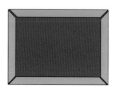

pet pages

materials
Colored pencils or pens
Handmade papers: coordinating
Lightweight paper: white
Magnetic sheet
Stickers

general supplies & tools
Adhesive
Craft knife
Scissors: craft

Note: All text for photo pages was typed on a computer using whimsical fonts and printed on various handmade papers. The papers were then gently torn from around the text.

The subject of all pictures was cut out from photographs using craft scissors. Small areas were cut out from photographs using a craft knife.

title page

instructions

1. Select a creative title and subtitle for page. Print titles on different handmade papers. Gently tear paper from around titles and adhere to page.

2. Cut out pet from photograph and adhere to page.

critter quiz

instructions

1. Create questions and fun facts that evoke memories of a pet. List multiple choice answers for each question and fact. Print questions and facts with multiple choice answers on handmade paper. Gently tear or cut paper from around words, leaving a ¼" margin all around.

2. Fold left margin at ¼" mark on each paper to create hinges. Adhere hinges to page.

3. Print letters of correct answers. Gently tear or cut paper from around letters. Adhere letters to album page, under corresponding questions and facts papers.

4. Use photographs and stickers to embellish album page as desired.

pet profile

instructions

1. Create a profile of fun and interesting facts and memories about a pet and its personality. List date of birth, identifying features, how the pet became a family member, etc. Print profile on handmade paper and gently tear paper from around profile. Adhere profile to album page.

2. Use close-up action photographs to embellish album page as desired.

More title ideas:
Dogs of Our Lives
The Guiding Dog
All My Critters
Pet Passion

tradition

instructions

1. Create a game from a family tradition such as "dress up." Print story of tradition on handmade paper. Gently tear paper from around story and adhere to page.

2. Adhere photograph to magnetic sheet and cut out.

3. Refer to small photograph on page 43. Draw items of clothing, such as a hat, vest, socks, or bandanna, to fit on pet photo using lightweight white paper and black pen. Color clothing with colored pencils or pens. Adhere clothing to magnetic sheet and cut out.

4. Cut an 8½ x 3¾ rectangle from a sheet of handmade paper. Fold as shown in **Diagram 1** to form an envelope. Adhere sides of envelope together. Adhere envelope to album page. Stuff envelope with clothing and pet magnets.

5. Use photographs depicting the tradition and stickers to embellish album page as desired.

Diagram 1

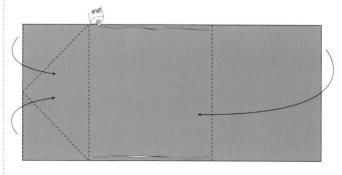

Add depth to a dark photograph by mounting it on a light-colored piece of paper, creating a silhouette effect.

shane game

instructions

1. Create a "concentration" game involving pets and critters. Cut an equal number of pairs of photographs or drawings of pets into square game pieces, or make two color copies of **Critters** below at a copy center and cut out.

2. Make appropriate number of symbols for top and bottom game pieces, or make color copies of **Symbols** provided below and on page 48. Adhere top and bottom symbols to magnetic sheet, making certain magnetic polarities match, and cut out.

3. Adhere back side of bottom game pieces in rows on album page. Adhere pet photographs/drawings to bottom side of top game pieces and place on top of bottom game pieces.

4. Print story and rules of game on handmade paper. Gently tear paper from around story and adhere to one side of album page.

5. Use photographs and stickers to embellish page.

Critters & Symbols

Symbols

Baby in Black & White

baby book

materials

Design materials: fabric, lace,
    ribbon, trims, etc.
Liquid gloss: polymer medium
    white
Paper: watercolor

general supplies & tools

Adhesive
Cardboard
Craft knife
Paintbrush

Ruler: metal edge
Scissors: craft; fabric

instructions

1. Design cover using desired
ribbons, laces, trims, fabrics, and

such. Tack design materials together and adhere to cardboard. Make a color copy of cover design at a copy center, reducing or enlarging to desired size. Trim color copy, if necessary, to fit top front cover using a craft knife and ruler.

2. Apply eight coats of gloss to color copy, allowing gloss to dry 30 minutes between coats. Allow final coat to dry 24 hours.

3. Soak coated paper in water until paper becomes soft enough to rub off. Remove all paper and rinse clean. Color remains with gloss forming a film. Let dry.

4. Cut watercolor paper same size as colored film.

5. Apply a coat of gloss to watercolor paper and adhere to bottom of colored film. Gently rub top of colored film to remove air bubbles and to seal edges, forming a cover.

6. Position cover on front of album and apply two coats of gloss, making certain edges are covered and sealed. Allow gloss to dry 24 hours.

7. Embellish as desired.

baby pages

Technique: Color small details on black-and-white photos or photo copies using pigment pens. Gently color details and immediately blot with paper towel to lighten color if desired.

general supplies & tools
Adhesive
Iron/ironing board
Pencil
Scissors: fabric

fabric photo mat

materials
Double-sided fusible web
Fabric: patchwork

instructions
1. Apply fusible web to back of fabric following manufacturer's instructions.

2. Cut fabric to fit album page. Cut out patches in fabric.

3. Lay fabric on album page and mark placement for photographs. Adhere photographs to album page.

4. Remove paper backing from fabric and iron onto album page, making certain iron does not touch photos.

materials

Ribbon: white organza; self-adhesive, coordinating colors and widths

instructions

1. Adhere photograph to album page.

2. Cut organza ribbon to fit over top of photograph.

3. Cut self-adhesive ribbons to form desired border and design around photograph and on album page. Adhere ribbons around photograph and to album page, making certain organza ribbon is secured over top of photo.

Take a photograph of the child each year, beginning at birth, with a stuffed animal to see how much the child has grown.

great-grandma

materials

Ribbon
Marker: fine point black

instructions

1. Adhere photo to album page.

2. Cut ribbon to form desired border around photo. Adhere ribbon to album page.

3. Label album page and draw decorative motifs using black marker.

Fabric Through the Year

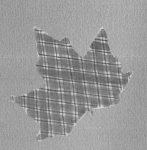

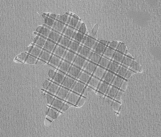

seasons

materials

Cardboard: lightweight

Cardstock

Dimensional fabric paint: coordinating (3)

Double-sided fusible web

Fabric: coordinating for cover; coordinating scraps (4)

Quilt batting: lightweight

general supplies & tools

Adhesive
Iron/ironing board
Pencil
Ruler
Scissors: craft; fabric

instructions

1. Lay album flat on work surface and measure. Cut a piece from quilt batting. Add 2" to height and width measurements and cut a piece from fabric for album cover.

2. Measure spine. Add 1⅛" to width and cut two strips from fabric. Adhere strips to inside spine, using an edge of a ruler to press fabric under metal ring plate.

3. Adhere quilt batting to album cover. Lay fabric wrong side up and center album over fabric. Wrap and adhere excess fabric to inside of binder, turning top and bottom edges under enough to fit up against edges of metal ring plate.

4. Cut cardboard into two pieces ¼" smaller than inside covers. Cut fabric into two pieces 1" larger than cardboard pieces. Lay fabric wrong side up and center cardboard on fabric. Wrap and adhere fabric edges to inside of cardboard. Adhere fabric-covered cardboard to inside front and back covers to hide all raw edges.

House Patterns

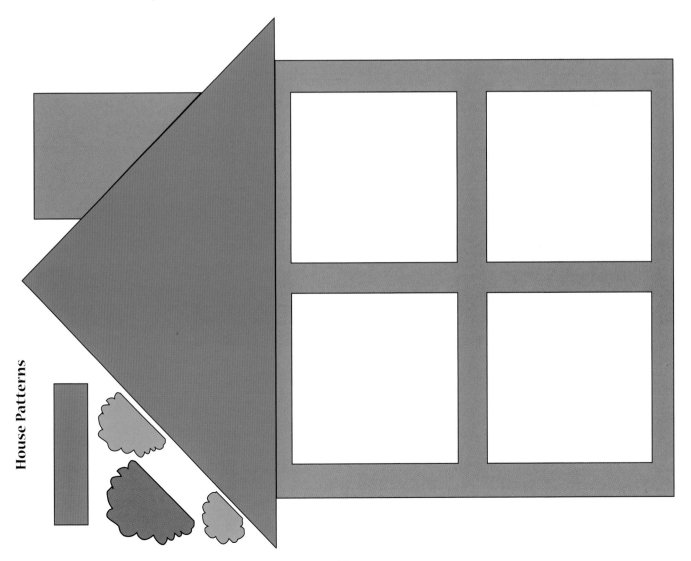

53

5. Refer to General Instructions for **Fusible Appliqué** on page 15. Reduce or enlarge **House Patterns** on page 53 and trace onto paper side of fusible web. Cut around motifs. Iron motifs to back sides of fabric scraps. Cut out motifs.

6. Remove paper backing from house motif and iron onto cardstock. Cut out house and windows using a craft knife and metal edge ruler.

7. Trim photographs to fit behind window openings and adhere in place. Adhere house to album cover. Cover house with a pressing cloth to avoid damaging photographs and fuse chimney to album cover. Fuse roof and shrubs to album cover.

8. With a decorative stitch, outline all edges of house pieces and shrubs and around edge of front cover using dimensional fabric paint. Allow paint to dry thoroughly.

valentine

materials
Cardstock: coordinating (3)
Decorative paper: coordinating (2)
Double-sided fusible web
Fabric: coordinating
Photo frames (2)

general supplies & tools
Adhesive
Craft knife
Iron/ironing board
Markers: fine tip black; metallic gold
Ruler: metal edge
Scissors: craft; decorative edge

instructions
1. Iron fusible web to back side of fabric following manufacturer's instructions. Remove paper backing and iron fabric to album page. Trim excess fabric from edges of album page using a craft knife and ruler.

2. Reduce or enlarge **Heart Patterns** below and on opposite page. Trace desired number of large and small hearts onto cardstock and decorative paper. Cut out hearts using decorative edge scissors. Trace medium hearts with lettering onto cardstock and trace over lettering using a black marker. Cut out medium hearts using craft scissors.

3. Center and trace frame opening onto photographs. Draw a ¼"-thick line around traced opening using a metallic gold marker.

4. Adhere photographs to photo frames. Adhere photo frames and hearts to album page.

Heart Patterns

bunny hop

materials
Acrylic paint: coordinating
Cardstock: coordinating (2)
Double-sided fusible web
Fabric: coordinating
Felt: coordinating
Ribbon: ⅛"-wide coordinating (5)

general supplies & tools
Adhesive
Craft knife
Iron/ironing board
Ruler: metal edge
Scissors: fabric; decorative edge
Stylus

instructions
1. Iron fusible web to back side of fabric following manufacturer's instructions. Remove paper backing and iron fabric to album page. Trim excess fabric from edges of album page using a craft knife and ruler.

2. Refer to General Instructions for **Fusible Appliqué** on page 15. Reduce or enlarge **Bunny Pattern** on page 56. Trace five bunnies onto paper side of fusible web. Cut around bunnies. Iron bunnies to felt and cut out using fabric scissors.

3. Cut one cardstock ⅛" larger than photograph using decorative edge scissors. Cut second cardstock ¼" larger than photograph. Center and adhere cardstocks together. Adhere photograph to cardstock.

4. Make a decorative dot pattern around border of photograph using stylus tip and acrylic paint.

5. Remove paper backing from bunnies and iron onto album page. Tie ribbons into small bows and adhere to bunnies.

6. Adhere photographs to album page.

Bunny Pattern

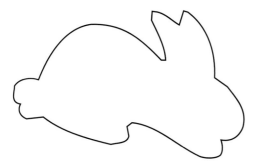

This bunny could also be used on a page dedicated to the family's pet rabbit.

pumpkin patch

materials
Cardstock: coordinating (3)
Double-sided fusible web
Fabric: coordinating Halloween prints (3)

general supplies & tools
Adhesive
Iron/ironing board
Marker: fine point black
Pencil
Scissors: craft; pinking shears

instructions
1. Iron fusible web to back side of one fabric following manufacturer's instructions.

2. Cut fabric ⅛" smaller than album page using pinking shears. Remove paper backing and iron fabric to album page.

3. Reduce or enlarge **Pumpkin Patterns** on page 58 and trace onto photos. Cut out photos using craft scissors.

4. Trace pumpkins onto two colors of cardstock. Cut out pumpkins ⅛" larger than cutting line.

5. Refer to General Instructions for **Fusible Appliqué** on page 15. Trace pumpkins and center pumpkin sections onto paper side of fusible web. Cut around pumpkins and sections. Iron pumpkins and center sections to back sides of remaining fabrics and cut out using fabric scissors. Remove paper backing and iron center pumpkin sections to pumpkins. Iron pumpkins to cardstock.

6. Adhere photographs to cardstock pumpkins.

7. Reduce or enlarge **Star & Moon Patterns** on opposite page and trace to cardstock and cut out using craft scissors.

8. Draw a decorative line around photographs, fabric pumpkins, stars, and moon using a black marker.

9. Adhere photographs, fabric pumpkins, stars, and moon to album page.

Star & Moon Patterns

pretty package

materials
Cardstock: coordinating (2)
Double-sided fusible web
Fabric: coordinating Christmas prints (2)

general supplies & tools
Adhesive
Craft knife
Iron/ironing board
Marker: fine point black
Paper punch
Ruler: metal edge
Scissors: craft; fabric; decorative edge

instructions
1. Iron fusible web to back side of one fabric following manufacturer's instructions. Remove paper backing and iron fabric to album page. Trim excess fabric from edges of album page using a craft knife and ruler.

2. Refer to General Instructions for **Fusible Appliqué** on page 15. Reduce or enlarge **Inside & Outside Package Patterns** on page 58. Trace outside package onto one cardstock and trace inside package onto paper side of fusible web. Cut out outside package using craft scissors. Cut around inside package. Iron inside package to back side of second fabric and cut out using fabric scissors. Remove paper backing and center and iron to outside package.

3. Cut four squares from second cardstock. Cut photographs ⅛" smaller than squares and adhere to squares. Adhere photo squares to package. Adhere package to album page.

4. Trace gift tag onto cardstock and cut out using decorative edge scissors. Outline gift tag and draw lettering using a black marker. Punch hole in end of gift tag. Adhere gift tag to package.

Pumpkin Patterns

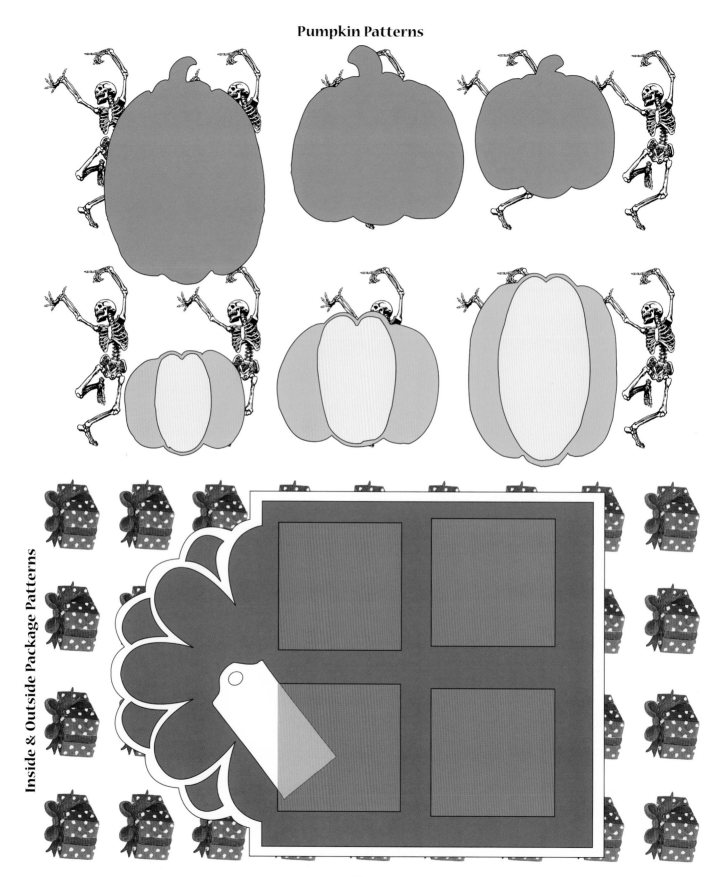

Inside & Outside Package Patterns

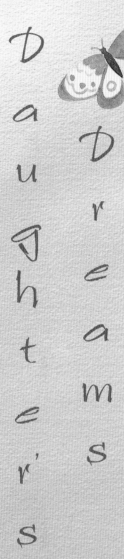

to my daughter

materials

Album: expandable spine
Buttons: ¼"–⅜" assorted coordinating (4)
Colored pencil: coordinating
Double-sided fusible web
Fabric: light-colored broadcloth;
    coordinating cotton; assorted
    coordinating scraps
Photo transfer paper: 8½" x 11"
Yarn: coordinating cotton crochet

general supplies & tools

Glue: fabric
Iron/ironing board
Measuring tape
Pressing cloth

Angel House   See page 63

Scissors: fabric
Sewing machine
Thread: coordinating

instructions

1. Measure an opened, flat album. Add ⅛" to height measurement and 11" to width measurement and cut piece from cotton fabric.

2. Press sides of short ends under ¼" and stitch a hem. With right sides together, fold short ends back 5¼". Stitch along top and bottom, from A to B, as shown in **Diagram 1**. Clip corners and turn right side out.

3. Turn remaining top and bottom edges under ¼" and stitch from B to B as shown in **Diagram 2**. Press.

4. Copy houses from **Angel House Artwork** on opposite page onto photo transfer paper at a copy center, following manufacturer's instructions. Reduce or enlarge as necessary.

5. Iron photo transfers onto broadcloth following manufacturer's instructions. Remove transfer while still hot.

6. Apply double-sided fusible web to back of broadcloth following manufacturer's instructions. Use a pressing cloth over top of photo transfers to prevent damage to transfers.

7. With a ⅛" margin, cut out each house.

8. Refer to General Instructions for **Fusible Appliqué** on page 15. Reduce or enlarge **Shapes Patterns** on page 63. Trace two hearts, stars, and flowers, and draw one rectangle for title box onto paper side of fusible web. Cut around motifs. Iron motifs to back sides of fabric scraps. Cut out motifs.

9. Refer to General Instructions for **Transferring** on page 18. Enlarge, center, and transfer **Daughter Verse** at right to title box using colored pencil.

10. Remove paper backing and arrange houses, motifs, and title box on front of album cover as desired. Lay pressing cloth over cover and iron pieces in place.

11. Draw stitch lines around inside edges of houses, motifs, and title box using colored pencil.

12. Cut two 2½" lengths and one 7" length from yarn. Knot one end of 2½" lengths and glue knotted end to center of each flower. Wrap and glue yarn in a spiral around knot. Tie 7" length into a bow with tails and glue to upper left corner of title box. Glue button on center of bow. Glue remaining buttons on lower right side of title box.

Diagram 1

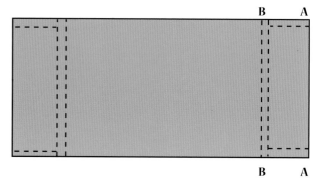

Diagram 2

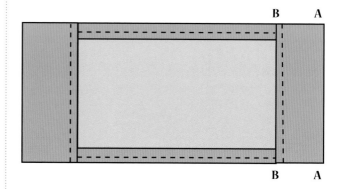

Daughter Verse   Enlarge 145%

60

Angels live with God, and sometimes they come to visit. They help love grow, but sometimes they can even chase away bad things. Angels have pretty names like Sistina and Auria. Some people say you become one when you die, but maybe we are all Angels now. What do you think? — Tatiana, age 8

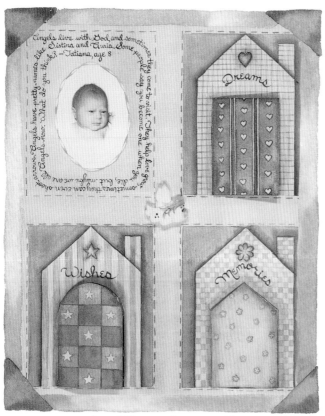

Angel House   See page 63

Butterfly Kisses   See page 63

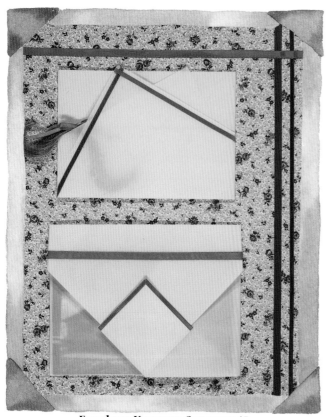

Envelope Keepers See page 65

Family Tree See page 66

Shapes Patterns

angel house

materials
Button: coordinating ceramic

general supplies & tools
Adhesive
Craft knife
Needle: hand-sewing
Ruler: metal edge
Thread: coordinating

instructions
1. Make a color copy of **Angel House Artwork** on page 61 at a color copy center, reducing or enlarging if necessary, to fit album page. Trim blank edges from around artwork using a craft knife and ruler.

2. Carefully cut around top, right side, and bottom of doors. Fold and crease left side of doors open.

3. With doors open, position and glue photographs to back of color copy. Cut photograph to fit top left frame on color copy and adhere in place.

4. Sew through button holes on ceramic button using needle and thread. Knot at back of button and glue to center of color copy. Adhere color copy to album page.

butterfly kisses

materials
Double-sided fusible web
Colored pencil: coordinating
Fabric: coordinating cotton

general supplies & tools
Adhesive
Cardboard: lightweight
Craft knife
Iron/ironing board
Pencil
Scissors: craft; fabric

instructions
1. Make a color copy of **Butterfly Artwork** on page 64 at a copy center, reducing or enlarging to desired size for album page. Cut out butterfly using a craft knife.

2. Reduce or enlarge **Butterfly Pattern** on page 65. Trace pattern onto cardboard and cut out for template.

3. Position template over each photograph and trace around template. Cut out photographs using craft scissors.

4. Apply double-sided fusible web to back of fabric following manufacturer's instructions. Measure and cut fabric to fit album page. Remove paper backing and iron fabric to album pages.

5. Arrange and adhere photographs and butterfly artwork to album pages as desired.

6. Draw stitch lines around photographs and artwork using colored pencil.

Today we would do well
to take a moment to dream
of lighthearted and sweet
beautiful things
like butterflies and daffodils,
and birds that sing.

Butterfly Pattern

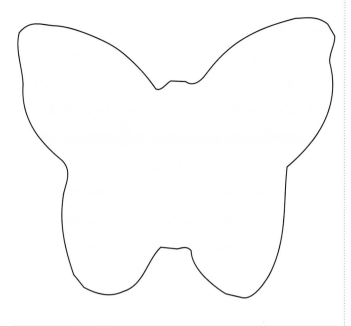

envelope keepers

materials

Embossing tool
Fabric: coordinating print
Ribbon: ⅛"-wide coordinating; ¼"-wide coordinating
Stencils: assorted as desired
Vellum paper: 11" x 17" white (2)

general supplies & tools

Adhesive
Craft knife
Iron/ironing board
Ruler: metal edge
Scissors

instructions

1. Press fabric. Make a color copy of fabric at a copy center, reducing or enlarging to desired size for album. Trim color copy, if necessary, to fit album page using a craft knife and ruler. Adhere color copy to album page.

2. Cut ¼"-wide ribbon into two lengths to fit across top and side of album page. Cut ⅛"-wide ribbon to fit across side of album page. Adhere ribbons in place as shown in photograph on page 62.

3. Fold right edge of one sheet of vellum paper to left edge as shown in **Diagram 1-A** on opposite page. Measure 4" from fold and fold again as shown in **B**. Measure 2¼" from upper left corner and fold to right as shown in **C**. Measure 2⅛" from upper right corner and fold to left as shown in **C**. Insert right end into fold of left end as shown in **D**.

4. Refer to General Instructions for **Embossing Paper** on page 15. Unfold envelope and position top flap, right side down, over stencil and rub embossing tool around edges of stencil. Stencil around inside edges of top flap.

5. Cut ⅛"-wide ribbon to fit edges of front flap of envelope. Adhere ribbons to envelope, ⅛" from edge, overlapping at top point.

6. Trim remaining sheet of vellum to 11" square and fold in half diagonally as shown in **Diagram 2-A** on page 66. Mark triangle into thirds along base and fold left corner over as shown in **B**. Fold right side over in same way as shown in **C**. Points and folds should meet. Fold back half of upper point as shown in **D**. Open small triangular section and flatten as shown in **E**. Fold down upper flap and insert into opened section as shown in **F**.

7. Position envelope flap right side down over stencil and gently but firmly press embossing tool around edges of stencil. Stencil across top edge of envelope flap.

8. Cut ¼"-wide ribbon to fit across top flap. Adhere ribbon to flap, slightly below embossed pattern.

9. Adhere envelopes to album page and tuck mementos inside.

Diagram 1

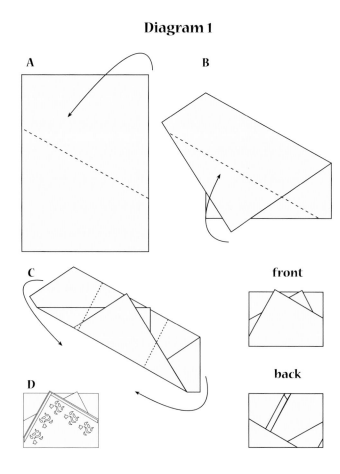

A   B

front

C   back

D

Diagram 2

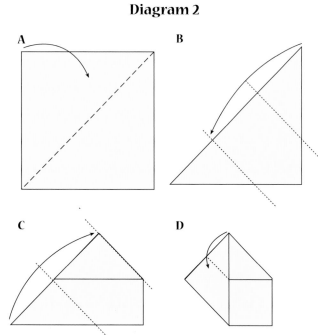

A   B

C   D

D (cont.)   E

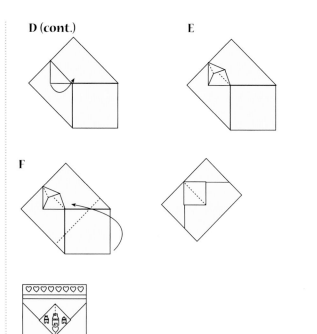

F

family tree

materials
Pigment pen: coordinating

general supplies & tools
Adhesive
Craft knife
Ruler: metal edge

instructions
1. Make desired number of color copies of **Family Tree Fruit** below and **Family Tree Artwork** on opposite page at a copy center, reducing or enlarging to desired size for album page.

2. Cut copy of family tree to fit album page using a craft knife and ruler. Adhere copy to album pages.

3. Write one family member name on each fruit using a pigment pen. Cut out, arrange, and adhere in order of pedigree.

Family Tree Fruit

high school days

materials
Binder: 3-ring
Charms or jacket pins (with pin cut off): assorted
Letterman's jacket emblems

general supplies & tools
Glue gun and glue sticks

instructions
1. Order name, year, and school insignia emblems from local letterman's jacket distributor.

2. Hot-glue emblems to front of binder as desired.

3. Hot-glue charms or pins to school insignia emblem.

alternate instructions

1. Cover binder with desired color fabric as instructed for **Seasons** Steps 1–4 on page 52. Order desired school emblem.

2. Cut the school letter out of cardboard and batting. Cover cardboard and batting letter with felt in the school color. Wrap and glue felt to back of cardboard.

3. Hot-glue letter and emblem to front of binder as desired.

high school pages

materials
Acrylic paints
Cardstock
Glitter
Paper: white transfer
Pens: pigment
Stickers

general supplies & tools
Adhesive
Craft knife
Marker: black permanent
Paintbrushes
Paint dishes
Paper towel
Pencil
Ruler: metal edge
Scissors: craft

instructions

1. Enlarge desired **Page Art** on pages 73–75 at a copy center, using colored cardstock of choice.

2. Depending upon pages selected, either cut out photo openings using a craft knife and ruler; trace photo slots onto transfer paper, transfer onto photographs, and cut out using craft scissors; or, cut photographs as desired to create a collage.

3. Use pigment pens or acrylic paints to color pattern pages. If painting, place three drops of paint into paint dish. Fill dish two-thirds full of water. Add additional drops of paint if deeper color is desired. Dip brush in paint then dab on paper towel to remove excess water. Allow paint to dry thoroughly. Place page under heavy object over night to avoid paper curl.

4. Adhere photographs to pattern pages.

5. Embellish pages with stickers and glitters as desired.

6. Label photographs and write narrative using a permanent marker.

$$2 \text{ good}$$
$$+ 2 \text{ be}$$
$$\overline{ 4 \text{ gotten}}$$

Friendly

EVENTS

Competition

MY LOCKER

VACATIONS

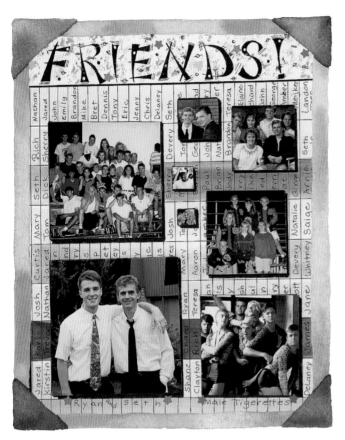

FRIENDS!

Ryan and Seth

Male Tigerettes

Track Team

Showtime OHS

Scott   Delaney   Seth

Sass and Dusty

Family and Friends

1996-1997

My Favorite Class...
Debate   Music
My Favorite
Teachers Mrs. Lee Mrs. Mason

SCHOOL

SENIOR MEMORIES

97

OGDEN HIGH SCHOOL

CONGRATULATIONS
DEBATE TEAM
STATE CHAMPIONS
ANOTHER STATE
TITLE FOR OHS

OGDEN HIGH SCHOOL

DEIA STATE CONVENTION
TELEMARKETING COMP
J FERRIN 2ND
FINALISTS
J OSWALD & A BARKER

Devery

Dad

John

Devery

Mom

'GRADUATION'
OH HAPPY DAY!

CLASS OF '92

DIFFERENT WALKS OF LIFE!

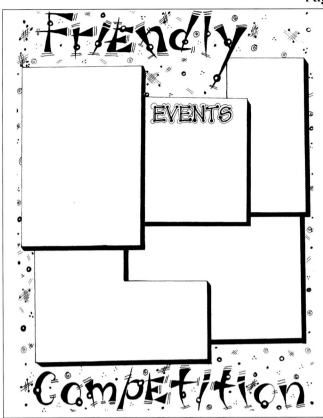

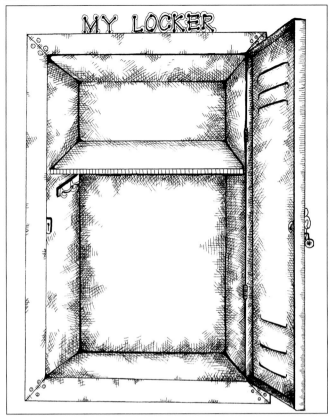

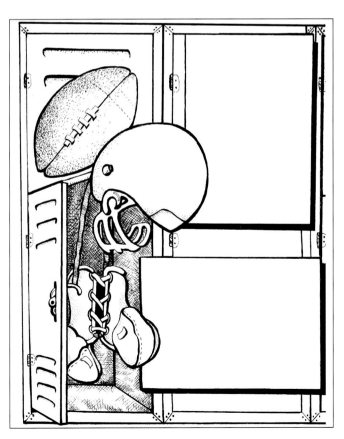

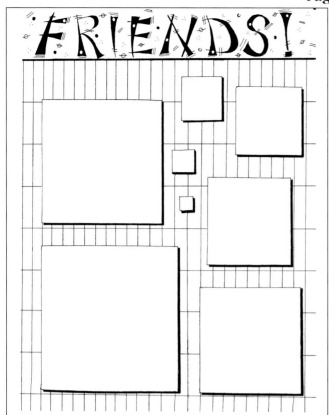

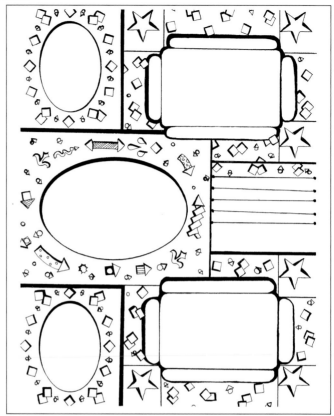

Accomplishments And Awards!

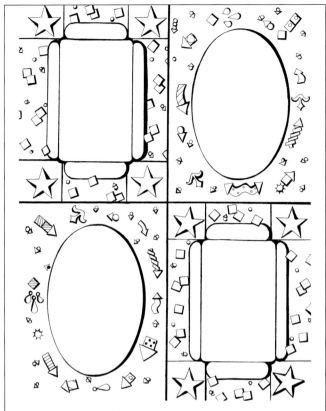

GRADUATION, OH, HAPPY DAY!

CLASS OF

DIFFERENT WALKS OF LIFE!

Weddings Are Forever

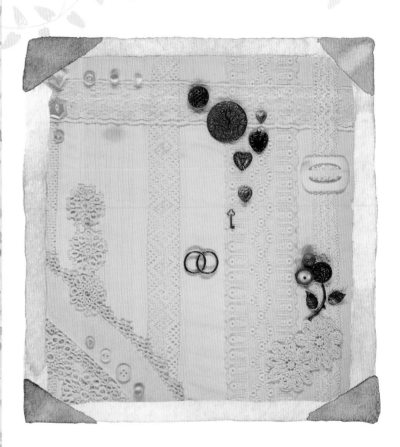

wedding album

materials
Album: expandable spine
Cardboard: lightweight
Embellishments: assorted buttons, buckles, charms,
    tatted pieces
Fabric: coordinating broadcloth
Gown: antique christening
Lace: assorted flat antique
Quilt batting: lightweight

general supplies & tools

Glue gun and glue sticks
Needle: hand-sewing
Scissors: fabric
Sewing machine
Straight pins
Thread: coordinating

instructions

1. Disassemble album. Measure front and back covers. Add 3" to height and width measurements and cut two pieces from gown and two pieces from broadcloth fabric.

2. Overlap one piece of gown on one piece of fabric ¼" and pin together for front. Sew two rows of stitches, ⅛" apart, using sewing machine. Repeat process for remaining gown and fabric pieces for back.

3. Embellish front cover with assorted buttons, buckles, charms, laces, and tatted pieces as desired. Tack all embellishments to cover using needle and coordinating thread.

4. Cut quilt batting to fit front and back covers. Hot-glue batting to top side of front and back covers.

5. Lay front and back fabric pieces face down. Center and lay covers on top of fabric, batting side down. Wrap and hot-glue fabric edges to inside of covers.

6. Wrap spine/page guard with lace and hot-glue to secure. Hot-glue lace over raw edges of inside binding folds on front and back covers. Cut holes in binding pieces for metal connectors to fit through.

7. Cut cardboard into two pieces, ⅛" smaller than inside covers. Cut fabric into two pieces, 1" larger than cardboard pieces. Lay cardboard onto fabric. Wrap and hot-glue fabric edges to inside of cardboard. Hot-glue fabric-covered cardboard to inside front and back covers to hide all raw edges.

8. Reassemble album.

wedding pages

general supplies & tools

Adhesive
Craft knife
Embossing tool
Light box
Ruler: metal edge
Scissors: craft; fabric
Stencil
Tape: drafting

weddings past

instructions

1. Make a color copy of **Antique Document** on page 78 at a copy center, reducing or enlarging if necessary, to fit album page. Trim color copy, if necessary, using a craft knife and ruler. Adhere color copy to album page.

2. Adhere photographs to album page as desired.

which said Messuages or Dwellinghouses Closes Lands Hereditam
piece or parcel of Land called the rough piece containing by estimat
Acre be the same more or less, One other piece or parcel of Land
parcels of Land Hereditaments and premises are situate lying
Ground AND ALSO One Barn and One Close called the Barn
Barn containing by estimation One Acre be the same more or
or less, One other Close called the Single containing by estima
estimation One acre and an half be the same more or less, O
or less, One other Close or parcel of Land called the Top
and Hereditaments are situate standing lying and being at
mentioned now are or late were in the tenure and Occupation
Undertenants Together with all and singular the Houses Out
ells Waters Watercourses Trees woods Underwoods Hedges Ditch
and Appurtenances whatsoever to the said Messuages Dwelling
wise appertaining Or accepted reputed taken and known as part
parcel thereof To have and to hold the said Messuages
bargained and sold with their Appurten
to the full end and term of
Thomas Flinn and George Flinn
that by virtue of these presents a
ession of the premises aforesaid with the Appurtenances And ma
ance thereof to him and his heirs To and for such Uses Estates
to bear date the day next after the day of the date hereof and
White of the other part by their several additions therein
als the Day and Year first above written.

cordially invited

materials

Cardstock: coordinating
Lace paper

instructions

1. Cut cardstock to fit album page using a craft knife and ruler. Adhere cardstock to album page.

2. Adhere lace paper at an angle to album page. Trim excess paper from edges of page using craft scissors.

3. Adhere invitations to album page as desired.

Make a color photocopy of completed album cover for excellent background paper for the rest of the photo pages.

generations

instructions

1. Make color copies of **Photo Surrounds** on page 80 at a copy center, reducing or enlarging to desired size for album page. Cut out photo surrounds using a craft knife and ruler. Cut out inside ovals and around flowers using a craft knife.

2. Position photographs in ovals and adhere to back of photo surrounds.

3. Refer to General Instructions for **Embossing Paper** on page 15. Position album page right side down over stencil on light box and tape page in place. Gently but firmly press around edges of stencil using embossing tool. Remove tape.

4. Adhere photo surrounds to album page as desired.

Poetry & Lace Photo Surround

Verse:

   A relationship is placing one's heart and soul in the hands of another while taking charge of another in one's soul and heart.

— Kahlil Gibran

4. Position photographs in openings and adhere to back of photo surround. Adhere photo surround to center of album page.

5. Glue lace around photo surround, leaving a space between photograph and lace same width as ribbon.

6. Cut four lengths from ribbon, two to fit vertically and two to fit horizontally on album page, using fabric scissors. Lay ribbons in space between photo surround and lace and adhere to album page using a small amount of craft glue in corners. Cut ribbon ends at an angle.

poetry & lace

materials

Cardstock: coordinating
Glue: craft
Lace: antique flat
Paper punch: decorative corner
Ribbon: coordinating

instructions

1. Make a color copy of **Poetry & Lace Photo Surround** on page 80 at a copy center, reducing or enlarging to desired size for album page.

2. Cut cardstock to fit album page using a craft knife and ruler. Adhere cardstock to album page. Punch top corners of photo surround using decorative paper punch.

3. Cut out center openings of photo surround using a craft knife and ruler.

art of marriage

instructions

Make a color copy of **Marriage Artwork** on page 83 at a copy center, reducing or enlarging if necessary, to fit album page. Trim color copy, if necessary, using a craft knife and ruler. Adhere color copy to album page.

garter photo corners

materials

Lace: 1"-wide gathered
Photo corners: clear
Ribbon: ¼"-wide coordinating

instructions

1. Cut lace into four equal lengths to fit diagonally around each corner of photograph. Wrap lace around corners and adhere to back of photograph.

2. Cut ribbon into four equal lengths to wrap around top edge of lace corners. Adhere ribbon to back of photograph.

3. Place clear photo corners on photograph and adhere to album page.

victorian house

instructions

1. Make a color copy of **Victorian Surround** on page 84 at a copy center, reducing or enlarging if necessary, to fit album page. Trim photo surround, if necessary, and cut out photograph openings using a craft knife and ruler.

2. Position photographs in openings. Trim photographs to reduce bulk from overlapping. Adhere photographs to back of photo surround.

3. Adhere photo surround to album page.

Verse:

Love for the joy of loving, and not for the offering of someone else's heart.

— Marlene Dietrich

The Art of Marriage

A good marriage must be created.

In the art of marriage the little things are the big things...
It is never being too old to hold hands.
It is remembering to say "I love you," at least once each day.
It is never going to sleep angry.
It is having a mutual sense of values and common objectives.
It is standing together facing the world.
It is forming a circle of love that gathers in the whole family.
It is speaking words of appreciation and
demonstrating gratitude in thoughtful ways.
It is having the capacity to forgive and forget.
It is in giving each other an atmosphere in which each can grow.
It is finding room for things of the spirit.
It is a common search for the good and the beautiful.
It is not only marrying the right partner,
It is being the right partner.

Wilferd A. Peterson

Victorian Surround

antiquity

materials

Album: expandable spine
Cardboard: lightweight
Charm: coordinating
Embroidery ribbon: 4mm
    coordinating; 13mm coordinating
Lace: ¼"-wide flat; 1½"-wide flat;
    medallions (4)
Leaf stems: velvet (2)
Organza ribbon: 24mm
    coordinating
Stamens: beaded (2)
Wire-edge ribbon: ⅝"-wide
    coordinating

general supplies & tools

Adhesive: solid; spray
Craft knife
Scissors: craft; fabric

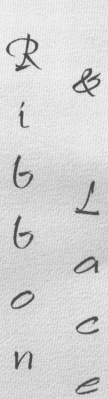

instructions

1. Disassemble album. Measure front and back covers. Add 3" to height and width measurements and cut two pieces from fabric using fabric scissors.

2. Spray top of front and back covers with adhesive. Center and lay covers on wrong side of fabric pieces. Wrap and adhere fabric edges to inside of covers. Cut out spine holes using a craft knife.

3. Cut cardboard into two pieces, ⅛" smaller than inside covers, using craft scissors. Cut fabric into two pieces, 1" larger than cardboard pieces. Center and lay cardboard on wrong side of fabric pieces. Wrap and adhere fabric edges to inside of cardboard. Adhere fabric-covered cardboard to inside front and back covers to hide all raw edges. Adhere ¼"-wide lace around edges of fabric-covered cardboard.

4. Adhere 1½"-wide lace around top edges of front cover. Adhere 4mm embroidery ribbon over edge of lace.

5. Enlarge **Oval Pattern** on page 87 at a copy center, to desired size for photograph (300% for original size). Trace oval onto cardboard and photograph and cut out using craft scissors. Spray cardboard with adhesive and adhere photograph to cardboard. Adhere photograph to center of album cover.

6. Adhere lace medallions around photograph. Adhere velvet leaves, beaded stamens, and charm to top of leaves as shown in photograph.

7. Refer to a ribbon embroidery instruction guide to do the following ribbonwork: a) make three freeform flowers using wire-edge ribbon; b) make three pencil flowers using 13mm embroidery ribbon; c) make one spiral rosetta using organza ribbon.

8. Adhere spiral rosetta on top of leaves and stamen as shown in photograph. Adhere freeform flowers and pencil flowers around spiral rosetta as desired.

9. Reassemble album.

Before cutting photos — photocopy!

family quilt

materials

Button: small
Double-sided fusible web
Embroidery floss: coordinating
Embroidery ribbon: 4mm
    coordinating;
    13mm coordinating
Fabric: assorted coordinating
    calico print scraps;
    white cotton, pressed
Lace: assorted flat scraps
Organza ribbon: 9mm
    coordinating;
    18mm coordinating
Photo transfer medium

general supplies & tools

Adhesive: fabric
Craft knife
Iron/ironing board
Needle: hand-sewing
Pencil
Ruler: metal edge
Scissors: fabric

instructions

1. Make a copy of photo and copies of **Quilt Patterns** below at a copy center, reducing or enlarging to desired size to fit album page.

2. Trace quilt pattern pieces onto paper side of fusible web. Cut around pattern pieces. Iron pattern pieces to back sides of fabric scraps. Add ¼" to all sides of pattern pieces and cut out.

3. Remove paper backing from fusible web and fuse pattern pieces to white cotton fabric, overlapping as necessary.

4. Transfer copy of photograph onto cotton fabric using photo transfer medium and following manufacturer's instructions. Enlarge, center, and trace **Oval Pattern** below onto fabric photo. Cut out fabric photograph. Adhere to center of "quilted" fabric.

5. Cut lace pieces to fit seams of "quilted" fabric and to fit around photo. Adhere lace to quilted fabric

6. Refer to an embroidery stitch guide to make the following stitches: randomly stitch lazy daisy petals along lace seams using a hand-sewing needle and two strands of embroidery floss.

7. Tie 4mm embroidery ribbon into a bow and glue to top center of oval, cascading ribbon tails around top portion of photo.

8. Refer to a ribbon embroidery stitch guide to do the following ribbonwork: a) make two freeform flowers using 13mm embroidery ribbon; b) make two gathered petals using 9mm organza ribbon; c) make six folded petals using 18mm organza ribbon.

9. Adhere folded petals in circle at top center of photo. Adhere button to center of petals. Adhere gathered petals on each side of petal flower. Adhere freeform flowers on each side of gathered petals.

10. Adhere "quilted" fabric to album page. If necessary, trim edges using a craft knife and ruler.

Quilt Patterns & Oval Pattern

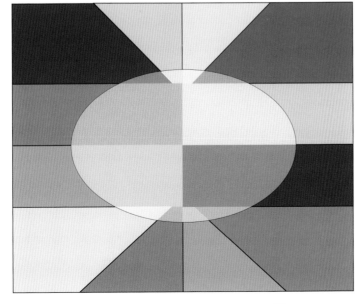
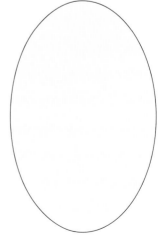

organandy envelope

materials

Cardboard: lightweight
Embroidery ribbon:
    7mm coordinating (2);
    13mm coordinating
Fabric: coordinating organza
Organza ribbon: 18mm
    coordinating;
Paper doily: 8" square
Picot-edge ribbon: ⅛"-wide
    coordinating
Spray paint: coordinating
Trim: coordinating eyelash

general supplies & tools

Adhesive: solid; spray
Craft knife
Pencil
Ruler: metal edge
Scissors: craft; fabric

instructions

1. Spray album page with spray paint. Let dry.

2. Spray album page with adhesive. Lay organza fabric over top and press to secure to album page. Trim excess fabric from edges of album page using a craft knife and ruler.

3. Adhere one 7mm embroidery ribbon around edge of album page. Adhere eyelash trim around edge of album page on top of embroidery ribbon.

4. Make a copy of **Small Oval Pattern** on opposite page at a copy center, reducing or enlarging to desired size. Trace two ovals onto cardboard and cut out using craft scissors.

5. Center and trace two ovals on photographs. Cut out.

Spray back of photographs with adhesive and adhere to cardboard ovals.

6. Refer to a ribbon embroidery stitch guide to do the following ribbonwork: a) make ⅛" box pleats along 13mm embroidery ribbon; sew a running stitch ⅛" from edge of ribbon; b) gather ribbon to fit around photographs; c) make three pencil flowers using one 7mm embroidery ribbon; d) make three baby rosettes using second 7mm embroidery ribbon.

7. Adhere ruched ribbons to edge of ovals. Cut two lengths from picot-edge ribbon to fit around outside edge of ovals. Adhere ribbon to top of ruched ribbons on ovals.

8. Cut three lengths from 18mm organza ribbon. Fold each ribbon as shown in **Diagram 1 (A–B)** and secure with adhesive. Cut three smaller lengths from 18mm organza ribbon and wrap a ribbon around each folded ribbon as shown in **C**, securing at back, to form a bow as shown in **D**. Adhere bow to center top of ovals. Set remaining bow aside.

9. Adhere baby rosettes in center of pencil flowers. Adhere one pencil flower to center top of each oval.

10. Cut 18mm organza ribbon into desired lengths for hangers. Fold ribbons in half and adhere raw ends to back of ovals. Adhere ovals to album page.

11. Fold paper doily into envelope as shown in Diagram 2 (A–E). Adhere three corners together.

Adhere remaining pencil flower to top of envelope flap.

12. Cut 18mm organza ribbon into desired length for envelope hanger. Adhere hanger to album page. Adhere envelope to album page at base of hanger. Adhere remaining organza bow to top of hanger.

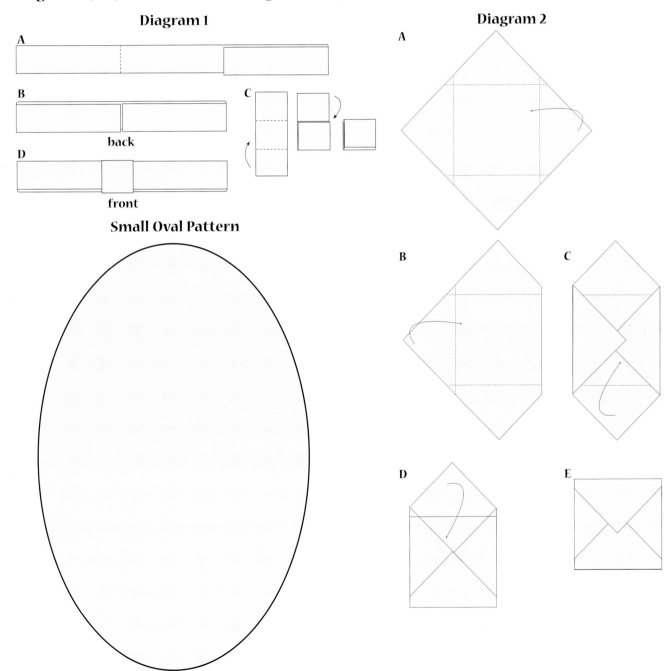

Diagram 1

Small Oval Pattern

Diagram 2

wedding vows

materials

Acrylic paints: coordinating (3)
Beads: coordinating seed (27)
Buttons: small (2)
Cardboard: lightweight
Cardstock: coordinating
Embroidery ribbon: 4mm coordinating;
5mm coordinating (2);
7mm coordinating (2)
Lace: ⅝"-wide flat
Trim: coordinating
Woven ribbon: 1½"-wide green
Wire-edge ribbon:
⅝"-wide coordinating (2);
⅞"-wide coordinating (2);
1½" -wide coordinating

general supplies & tools

Adhesive; solid; spray
Craft knife
Paint roller brush: small
Pen: gold
Pencil
Ruler: metal edge
Scissors: fabric; decorative edge
Sponge
Transfer paper

instructions

1. Paint album page using a small roller brush and one color of paint. Apply remaining colors of paint, one at a time, using a sponge. Allow paint to dry.

2. Make a copy on cardstock of **Oval with Verse** on opposite page at a copy center. Cut out oval using decorative edge scissors and leaving a ⅛" border. Color decorative border around oval using a gold pen.

3. Spray cardboard with adhesive. Adhere photographs to cardboard and cut out using a craft knife and ruler. Adhere photographs to album page.

4. Adhere lace around photographs, mitering corners. Adhere trim on top of lace at edge of photographs.

5. Refer to General Instructions for **Transferring** on page 18. Transfer desired number of leaves onto green ribbon using **Leaf Pattern** on opposite page and transfer paper. Trace over transfer lines with a gold pen and cut out leaves using fabric scissors. Adhere leaves to album page as desired.

6. Cut 5mm embroidery ribbon into desired length to cascade across top of photographs. Randomly tie knots in ribbon and knot ribbon ends. Adhere ribbon to album page.

7. Refer to a ribbon embroidery instruction guide to do the following ribbonwork: a) stitch one ruched ribbon flower using ⅞"-wide wire-edge ribbon; b) stitch one multi-petal flower with tucks using ⅝"-wide wire-edge ribbon; c) stitch one double ruffle rosette using 1½"-wide wire-edge ribbon; d) fold and stitch three pansies using ⅝"-wide wire-edge ribbon with 7mm embroidery ribbon for centers; e) make desired number of pencil flowers using 4mm and 7mm embroidery ribbons; sew three seed beads in center of each pencil flower.

8. Adhere flowers to album page as shown in photograph. Adhere buttons in center of folded multi-petal flower and double ruffle rosette.

Leaf Pattern

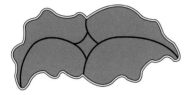

Oval with Verse Enlarge 125%

Let me dwell in the light of thine eyes, Let me find a sweet home in thy heart! For my soul like a wild bird flies, To linger wherever thou art—As night gives place to the day, And darkness before the sun flies, So my sorrows will all melt away, When I live in the light of thine eyes.

grandma's fan

materials
Acrylic paints: coordinating (2)
Cardboard: lightweight
Charms: coordinating (3)
Cording: ⅛"-wide coordinating
Double-sided fusible web
Embroidery ribbon: 13mm
    coordinating
Fabric: coordinating; lace
Organza ribbon: 5mm
    coordinating;
      9mm coordinating;
      18mm coordinating, green;
      24mm coordinating
Picot-edge ribbon: ⅛"-wide
    coordinating
Spray paint: coordinating
Wallpaper: coordinating print

general supplies & tools
Adhesive: archival; fabric; spray
Iron/ironing board
Marking pen
Paint brush: large flat
Pencil
Sealer: matte spray
Scissors: craft; decorative edge; fabric

instructions
1. Spray album page using light coat of spray matte sealer. Let dry. Spray album page with light coat of adhesive. Let dry. Lay lace fabric over top of album page and lightly spray lace and album page using spray paint. Lift lace and let painted album page dry.

2. Mix water with each acrylic paint in a 3:1 ratio. Wash painted album page with each. Let dry.

3. Make a copy of **Fan Patterns** at right and on opposite page at a copy center, reducing or enlarging to desired size to fit album page. Trace fan blade, frame, and two ovals onto cardboard and cut out with craft scissors. Set ovals aside for Step 7.

4. Trace seven blades (one next to the other) onto cardboard to form complete fan. Trace seven blades onto back of wallpaper using fan blade template. Spray back of wallpaper with spray adhesive and cut out blades. Attach paper blades to cardboard fan. Trim fan edge with decorative edge scissors.

5. Cut picot-edge ribbon into eight lengths for spokes of fan. Adhere ribbon to fan using fabric glue. Adhere completed fan to album page. Adhere large charm to bottom of fan.

6. Trace frame onto fusible web, adding ⅛ to inside cutting line. Cut out traced frame from fusible web, leaving center uncut, and fuse to fabric. Add ⅛ to outside cutting line and cut out traced frame from fabric. Spray cardboard frame with adhesive. Place sprayed side of frame onto fused web. Clip curves on fabric. Wrap fabric to back of frame and secure using fabric glue.

7. Trace oval from center of cardboard frame onto two photographs. Enlarge oval by ⅛ and trace onto third photograph and cardboard. Cut out oval photographs and cardboard oval using craft scissors. Spray adhesive onto photographs and adhere to cardboard ovals.

8. Refer to a ribbon embroidery instruction guide to do the following ribbonwork: a) make nine folded petals using 13mm embroidery ribbon and adhere three petals to top backside of each small oval and to top backside of frame; b) make eight folded petals using 18mm organza ribbon and adhere four petals each to top backside of small ovals; c) make twelve folded petals using green organza ribbon and adhere three petals each to backside of small ovals and,

rather than gluing ends flat on remaining six petals, pinch and glue ends, cutting off excess tails and adhering to front of frame for leaves; d) make five folded petals using 24mm organza ribbon and adhere to back of petals on frame; e) make three pencil flowers using 9mm organza ribbon and adhere one flower to front of each small charm and to front of frame; f) make one pencil flower using 5mm organza ribbon and adhere to front of frame; g) make one circular ruffle using 13mm embroidery ribbon and adhere to front of frame.

9. Cut cording into two lengths to fit around front edge of each small oval. Adhere cording to ovals. Adhere one small charm with pencil flower to each small oval.

10. Adhere small ovals to album page. Adhere large oval to back of frame. Adhere frame to album page.

Fan Patterns

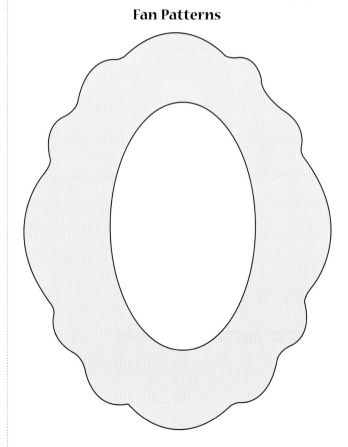

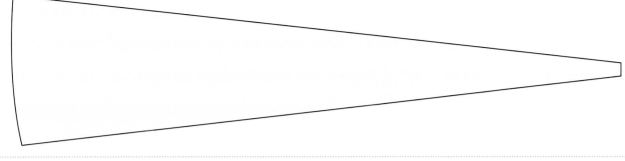

fuchsia frames

materials

Acrylic paint: coordinating
Buttons: small assorted (3)
Dowel: ⅛" x 36"
Embroidery ribbon: 4mm
      coordinating; 13mm coordinating
Fabric: coordinating moiré
Lace: ¼"-wide flat
Ribbon: ⅞"-wide coordinating (3);
      1½"-wide coordinating
Stamens

general supplies & tools

Adhesive: solid; spray
Craft knife
Paintbrush
Ruler: metal edge
Scissors: fabric

instructions

1. Apply spray adhesive to album page. Center and adhere fabric to album page. Let dry. Trim excess fabric from edges of album page using a craft knife and ruler.

2. Adhere lace around edge of album page.

3. Cut dowel to create frames for photos as shown in photograph. Paint dowel pieces with paint and let dry. Adhere photographs to album page. Adhere dowel pieces around photographs.

4. Refer to a ribbon embroidery stitch guide to do the following ribbonwork: a) make three fuchsias using one ⅞"-wide ribbon, two using second ⅞"-wide ribbon, two using remaining ⅞"-wide ribbon, and one using 1½"-wide ribbon; b) make three freeform flowers using 13mm embroidery ribbon.

5. Randomly tie knots on a length of 4mm green embroidery ribbon and cascade ribbon across top of photo frames. Adhere to album page at knots.

6. Adhere ribbon flowers to album page as desired above photo frames. Adhere buttons in centers of freeform flowers.

trellis

materials

Cardboard: lightweight
Embroidery ribbon: 7mm coordinating
Fabric: lace netting
Organza ribbon: 24 mm
     coordinating (2);
     18 mm coordinating, green
Paper cutouts
Spray paint: coordinating

general supplies & tools

Adhesive: solid, spray
Craft knife
Ruler: metal edge

instructions

1. Paint album page using spray paint.

2. Spray album page with adhesive. Lay lace netting over top and press to secure to album page. Trim excess netting from edges of album page using a craft knife and ruler.

3. Cut embroidery ribbon into desired number of lengths to fit across album page in a trellis pattern as shown in photograph. Adhere ends of ribbons to album page.

4. Spray cardboard with adhesive. Adhere photographs to cardboard and cut out using a craft knife and ruler. Slip photographs under and over trellis and adhere in place.

5. Cut green organza ribbon into two lengths. Twist ribbons into stems and adhere to album page.

6. Refer to a ribbon embroidery instruction guide to do the following ribbonwork: a) stitch three free form flowers using one 24mm organza ribbon; b) stitch three free form flowers using second 24mm organza ribbon and three using 18 mm organza ribbon; c) fold and stitch twenty-six folded leaves using remaining 18 mm green organza.

7. Assemble all flowers in the following manner: place flower inside one leaf and secure with adhesive; place end of leaf inside a second leaf and secure with adhesive; place end of second leaf inside a third leaf and secure with adhesive. Adhere flowers and leaves to album page.

8. Embellish album page with paper cutouts as desired.

9. Adhere remaining embroidery ribbon around edges of album page.

Verse:

Those who bring sunshine to the lives of others cannot keep it from themselves.

— Sir James M. Barrie

sister's favorite

materials

Beads: coordinating seed (3)
Buttons: small (2)
Cardstock: coordinating
Charms
Embroidery ribbon: 4mm
    coordinating (2);
    13mm coordinating (4)
Fabric: sheer
Lace: ¼"-wide flat
Wrapping paper: coordinating

general supplies & tools

Adhesive
Craft knife
Ruler: metal edge
Scissors: fabric; decorative edge

instructions

1. Adhere wrapping paper to album page. Trim excess paper from edges of album page using a craft knife and ruler.

2. Place a thin layer of adhesive around edges of album page. Lay sheer fabric over top and adhere to album page. Trim excess fabric from edges of album page. Adhere lace around edges of album page.

3. Adhere photographs to cardstock, leaving 1" between photographs. Cut out photographs on cardstock using decorative edge scissors and leaving a ¼" border. Adhere photographs to album page as desired.

4. Refer to a ribbon embroidery instruction guide to do the following ribbonwork: a) stitch two pansies using one 13mm embroidery ribbon; b) fold and glue five folded petals using second 13mm embroidery ribbon; c) stitch three freeform flowers using third 13mm embroidery ribbon; sew seed beads in center of one flower; fold remaining flowers in half; d) stitch one pencil violet using fourth embroidery ribbon; e) stitch three pencil violets using 4mm embroidery ribbon.

5. Cut second embroidery ribbon into desired lengths to cascade around photographs. Randomly tie knots in ribbons. Tie charms onto ribbons as desired. Adhere ribbons around photographs as desired.

6. Adhere ribbon flowers in corners of photographs, on top of cascading ribbons. Adhere folded petals in a circle on corner of one photograph. Adhere buttons in center of 13mm pencil violet and folded petal flower.

Use new or antique victorian-looking frames to create quick photo frames to decorate old family photographs. Place the frames upside down on a copy machine set "darker" and copy. Trace the copy onto a fine quality piece of paper, using a brown or black pigment pen. Cut out the frame and place it on a patterned background paper.

days gone by

materials

Acrylic paints: coordinating colors (2), copper, gold

Cardboard: lightweight

Charms: coordinating

Decoupage medium: matte

Double-sided fusible web

Fabric: coordinating tapestry

Leaf: fabric

Paper: coordinating decorative

Photo album: 3-ring binder

Photo mat: pre-cut

Ribbon: ¾"-wide coordinating wire-edge ombré; 1½"-wide coordinating wire-edge ombré

general supplies & tools

Adhesive
Iron/ironing board
Paintbrush
Pencil
Scissors: craft; fabric
Sponge

instructions

1. Paint photo album with two light coats of decoupage medium mixed 1:1 with water. Let dry.

2. Lightly sponge several layers of acrylic paint on album, beginning with darkest coordinating color and finishing with copper and gold. Let dry.

3. Paint two more layers of decoupage medium thinned with water over sponged album. Let dry.

4. Highlight fabric leaf with copper and gold paints. Paint edge of leaf and edge of photograph gold.

5. Adhere 1½"-wide wire-edge ribbon down left side of album, ⅛" from edge. Wrap ends around to inside of cover and secure.

6. Cut tapestry fabric 1" larger than photo mat. Cut fusible web same size as mat. Mark opening with pencil and cut out using fabric scissors.

7. Following manufacturer's instructions, adhere fusible web to photo mat. Remove paper backing and adhere fabric to mat.

8. Cut out opening in fabric, leaving a 1" border. Clip around opening every 1" and to within ⅛" of mat. Fold flaps to wrong side of mat opening and secure with adhesive.

9. Cut cardboard same size as photo mat. Adhere decorative paper to cardboard and then adhere photograph, making certain photograph placement fits photo mat opening. Adhere mat and photo boards

together. Place under a heavy object until adhesive is thoroughly dry.

10. Wrap and adhere ¾"-wide ombré ribbon around left side of photo mat, securing at back of mat. Adhere fabric leaf in top left corner of mat. Tie ¾"-wide ombré ribbon into a bow with tails. Adhere bow on top of leaf, cascading tails as desired. Adhere charms to leaf and bow. Adhere embellished photo mat to album cover.

textured pages

Follow instructions for each page in this section or obtain color photo copies, enlarged to desired size, of the textured pages provided on pages 104–107.

Use a craft knife and ruler to carefully cut out photographs on copies, leaving photo openings. Place personal photographs behind photo openings and adhere to back of color copy. Mount copy to cardstock.

little sister

materials

Acrylic paints: coordinating; gold
Embellishments: coordinating
Paper: handmade ovals (see **Handmade Paper Ovals** on page 16); marbled (see **Marbling Paper** on page 16); sponged (see **Sponging Paper** on page 18)
Stencils: coordinating; decorative edge

general supplies & tools

Adhesive
Paintbrushes
Paper towels
Scissors: craft
Sponges: 1"–2"-wide, sea

instructions

1. Mark pattern on edge of marbled paper using a decorative edge stencil. Cut pattern edge.

2. Stencil design on handmade paper oval using coordinating acrylic paint and sponge. Load sponge with paint (or mixture of paints). Dab excess paint onto paper towel to avoid seepage under stencil. Softly pat stencil in an up-and-down motion over stencil. Remove stencil and let paint dry.

3. Stencil design on marbled paper.

4. Paint edges of marbled paper, photograph, and embellishments using gold paint.

5. Adhere paper oval to stenciled, marbled paper. Adhere photograph to paper oval. Adhere stenciled, marbled paper to a sheet of sponged paper. Adhere embellishments as desired.

Say "thank you" to a special teacher by making up an album chronicling the school year.

pansy border

materials

Acrylic paints: coordinating; gold
Cardstock: coordinating
Charms (4)
Clipart border
Colored pencils: soft-leaded
Greeting card: coordinating
Grosgrain ribbon: ⅛"-wide coordinating
Photo mounts: gold corner (4)
Wire-edge ribbon: ¾"-wide coordinating

general supplies & tools

Adhesive
Glue gun and glue sticks
Paintbrushes
Scissors: craft
Toothpicks: round

instructions

1. Make a photo copy of a clipart border design using brown tones at a copy center. Cut out one side of design to form a decorative corner border.

2. Lightly color details on border design using colored pencils. Repeat, building light layers of color. Do not work in one heavy layer.

3. Paint background area of border design and a ¼"-wide border around photograph using acrylic paint.

4. Cut desired motifs from greeting card.

5. Paint edges of motifs, border, and photograph, and add detailing on border design using gold paint. Lightly dot gold paint around design areas using toothpicks.

6. Adhere corner border design and photograph to cardstock.

7. Cut a length from wire-edge ribbon 2" longer than length of album page. Gently pull wires to remove from ribbon edges. Adhere ribbon to left edge of cardstock.

8. Cut four 4" lengths from wire-edge ribbon. Shape each ribbon into a fan and secure with a dot of hot glue. Adhere fans to corners of photograph. Hot-glue charms to ribbon fans.

9. Cut three lengths from grosgrain ribbon to fit across top, bottom, and right side of cardstock. Adhere ribbons to cardstock.

10. Attach photo corners to corners of cardstock. Adhere cardstock to album page.

For a 50th wedding anniversary, send a scrapbook page to friends of the couple. Have them include a photo and write down a memory.

train

materials

Cardboard: lightweight
Embellishments: coordinating
Paper: coordinating color; patterned paper using plastic wrap and watercolors (see **Plastic Wrap Painting** on page 17) (2); sponged paper (see **Sponging Paper** on page 18); marbled paper (see **Marbling Paper** on page 16)
Silhouette pattern

general supplies & tools

Adhesive
Craft knife
Masking tape
Newspapers
Paintbrush
Ruler: metal edge

instructions

1. Place silhouette pattern face up on colored paper and tape edges together.

2. Cut out silhouette pattern from colored paper using a craft knife and newspapers as a pad. If there are openings at center of pattern, cut these first and cut outside edges last.

3. Thin adhesive to a brushable consistency. Brush on backside of colored silhouette, brushing from center to outside edges.

4. Adhere silhouette to patterned paper. Surface may be lightly sponged with a damp cloth to remove excess adhesive.

5. Cut out center of sponged paper, using a craft knife and ruler, to create a ⅛"-wide frame. Adhere frame to patterned paper.

6. Adhere photograph to leftover sponged paper. Trim paper to a ⅛" border around photograph. Adhere photograph to patterned paper.

7. Adhere embellishments to patterned paper as desired.

ship

materials
Cardboard: lightweight
Gold leafing
Gold leafing adhesive
Paper: coordinating color; patterned paper using plastic wrap and watercolors (see **Plastic Wrap Painting** on page 17); marbled paper (see **Marbling Paper** on page 16)
Photo mounts: gold corner (4)
Silhouette pattern

general supplies & tools
Adhesive
Craft knife
Masking tape
Newspapers
Paintbrush
Ruler: metal edge

1. Repeat **Train** Steps 1-4 above using silhoutte pattern.

2. Cut two ⅛"-wide strips of marbled paper to fit across top and bottom of remaining sheet of patterned paper. Adhere strips to patterned paper.

3. Adhere gold photo mounts in corners of patterned paper.

4. Cut cardboard ⅛" larger than photograph. Adhere photograph to cardboard.

5. Cut leftover marbled paper into a ¼"-wide frame to fit around photograph. Adhere frame to cardboard. Adhere framed photograph to patterned paper as desired.

6. Apply gold leafing to corners of framed photograph following manufacturer's instructions.

dear friends

materials
Acrylic paint: gold
Cardstock: coordinating
Leaves: velvet (3)
Paper: sponged (see **Sponging Paper** on page 18)
Photo corners: decorative (4)
Postcard: coordinating
Ribbon: ⅛"-wide coordinating
Stickers

general supplies & tools
Adhesive
Craft knife
Hot glue gun and glue sticks
Paintbrush
Waxed paper

instructions
1. Enlarge postcard to desired size for album page at a photocopy center.

2. Cut a decorative opening in postcard using a craft knife.

3. Lay postcard on waxed paper and outline opening with a bead of hot glue. Let adhesive dry and then paint glue with gold acrylic paint. Outline details on postcard, if desired. Remove waxed paper.

4. Paint edges of postcard, leaves, and stickers by loading paintbrush with gold acrylic paint and using a scraping motion. Let dry for one hour.

5. Center and adhere photograph over opening on back side of postcard. Adhere postcard to sponged paper. Adhere stickers and leaves to postcard.

6. Tie ribbon into a bow and adhere to postcard.

7. Adhere sponged paper to cardstock for album page. Adhere decorative photo corners to album page.

A scrapbook makes a priceless gift for a best friend's birthday. Gather photographs of times shared throughout the years. Include event tickets or programs from concerts, plays, games, and other activities that friends attended together. Write about favorite past-times and experiences that should not be forgotten.

special delivery

materials
Acrylic paints: brown, gold
Cardstock: light colored (1), dark colored (2)
Charms: coordinating (3)
Envelope: decorative coordinating
Paper cut-outs: decorative coordinating
Ribbon: ⅛"-wide coordinating; ⅜"-wide coordinating

general supplies & tools
Adhesive
Paintbrush
Paper towels
Scissors: paper edgers

instructions
1. Trim one dark-colored cardstock to 7" x 10" and other to 3½" x 5½" using paper edgers.

2. Crumple envelope and carefully tear edges for a tattered appearance. Smooth envelope and brush with clean water to dampen.

3. Add one drop of brown acrylic paint to one tablespoon of water. Stir with paintbrush until water and paint are well mixed. Brush onto envelope, allowing paint-stained water to sink into broken areas of envelope. Immediately blot with paper towel. Repeat process as desired.

4. Adhere ⅛"-wide ribbon down left side of light-colored cardstock.

5. Load paintbrush with gold acrylic paint and paint edges of all pieces of cardstock and paper cut-outs in a scraping motion. Drybrush broken areas on envelope and on small dark colored cardstock with gold acrylic paint. Allow paint to dry for approximately one hour.

6. Adhere large dark-colored cardstock to light-colored cardstock, and adhere envelope to cardstock, positioning as desired.

7. Adhere ⅛"-wide ribbon across tops of cardstock. Tie ⅜"-wide ribbon into a bow and adhere to envelope.

8. Adhere photograph to small dark-colored cardstock and position in envelope. Secure with adhesive. Adhere paper cut-outs inside envelope.

9. Adhere charms in top corners of photograph and on knot of bow.

Honor a family heritage by displaying a family crest (if available), the meaning of the surname, a map of the country where the family originated, photographs or postcards of that country or people, and important holidays or events that may still be passed on through the family that originated in the old country.

3. Layer and adhere decorative tissue paper over top of cardstocks.

4. Tear random shapes from oriental lace paper. Randomly and sparingly apply adhesive to layered tissue paper and press lace paper onto layered tissue paper. Set several torn pieces aside.

5. Apply adhesive to back of photograph and adhere to layered paper. Adhere remaining torn pieces of lace paper around photograph.

6. Tie ribbon into a bow and adhere at bottom of photograph.

oriental lace

materials
Acrylic paint: gold
Cardstock: black, white
Paper: oriental lace; decorative tissue
Photo: hand-tinted (see **Hand-tinting Photographs** on page 16.)
Ribbon: ¾"-wide coordinating

general supplies & tools
Adhesive
Paintbrush
Scissors: paper edgers

instructions
1. Trim white cardstock to 8¼" x 10¾" using paper edgers.

2. Paint two coats of gold acrylic paint on side of white cardstock. Center and adhere gold-painted cardstock to black cardstock.

mother & daughter

materials
Acrylic paint: coordinating, brown, gold
Cardstock

Leaf: fresh, natural
Paper: white ; oriental
Ribbon: ¼-wide
Rosettes: coordinating (8)

general supplies & tools

Adhesive
Paintbrush
Paper edgers

instructions

1. Crinkle white paper and carefully tear edges for a tattered appearance. Smooth paper and brush with clean water to dampen.

2. Add one drop of brown acrylic paint to one tablespoon of water. Stir with paintbrush until water and paint are well mixed. Brush onto paper, allowing paint-stained water to sink into broken areas of paper. Immediately blot with paper towel. Repeat process as desired. Adhere crinkled paper to cardstock.

3. Adhere ribbon to left side of cardstock.

4. Trim photograph using paper edgers and adhere to crinkled paper.

5. Paint underside of leaf with acrylic paints. Press oriental paper onto leaf and gently smooth paper with fingers from center to outside edges, pressing paint and image into paper. Lift paper and let dry to touch. Trace around outside edge of leaf print with paintbrush and clear water. Reload paintbrush with water as necessary. Gently tear leaf print from paper at dampened edge. Allow edges to dry.

6. Thin adhesive with water and apply to backside of leaf print. Adhere leaf print to crinkled paper, overlapping edges onto photograph.

7. Adhere rosettes to top corners of photograph and randomly to leaf print.

Little Sister Art

Mother & Daughter Art

Pansy Border Art

Train Art

Ship Art

Dear Friends Art

Special Delivery Art

Oriental Paper Art

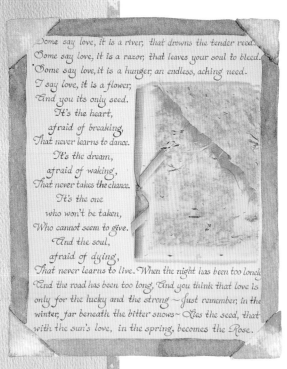

Some say love, it is a river, that drowns the tender reed.
Some say love, it is a razor, that leaves your soul to bleed.
Some say love, it is a hunger, an endless, aching need.
I say love, it is a flower,
And you its only seed.
It's the heart,
afraid of breaking,
That never learns to dance.
It's the dream,
afraid of waking,
That never takes the chance.
It's the one
who won't be taken,
Who cannot seem to give.
And the soul,
afraid of dying,
That never learns to live. When the night has been too lonely
And the road has been too long, And you think that love is
only for the lucky and the strong ~ Just remember, in the
winter, far beneath the bitter snows~ Lies the seed, that
with the sun's love, in the spring, becomes the Rose.

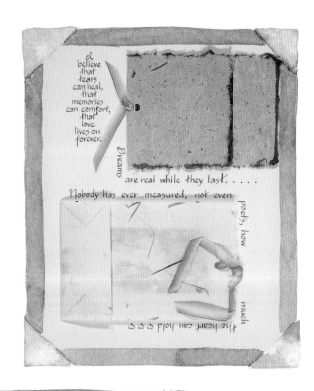

I believe that tears can heal, that memories can comfort, that love lives on forever.

Dreams are real while they last. . . . .

Nobody has ever measured, not even poets, how much the heart can hold.

Sentimental
Journey

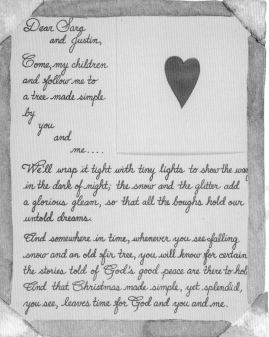

Dear Sara
and Justin,

Come, my children
and follow me to
a tree made simple
by
you
and
me....

We'll wrap it tight with tiny lights to show the way
in the dark of night; the snow and the glitter add
a glorious gleam, so that all the boughs hold our
untold dreams.

And somewhere in time, whenever you see falling
snow and an old fir tree, you will know for certain
the stories told of God's good peace are there to hold.
And that Christmas made simple, yet splendid,
you see, leaves time for God and you and me.

sentimental pages

instructions

Turn favorite greeting cards into photo mats. Use adhesive tape to attach photographs to mats.

Place photographs inside small paper books and envelopes.

Write a favorite message, poem, or thought using a coordinating calligraphy pen.

for giving, for sharing... laughter...
are our Joy
Our affections

Keep love in your life my child—
If you would have perfec

The face of all
the world changed
when first I heard
the footsteps
of your souls.

DESTINY

Those Who
Hear Not
The Music

Think The
Dancers
Mad.

Some reckon
time by stars,
And some by
hours;
Some measure
days by dreams,
And some by
flowers;
My heart alone
records
All our days
and hours.

VANESSA ANN COLLECTIBLES

You are a part of lovliness to me

whatever is honorable, whatever is just, whatever is pure, whatever is lovely, whatever is gracious, if there is any excellence, whatever is true, whatever is anything worthy of praise, think about these things. Philippians 4:8 In the language of flowers, pansies mean Thoughts.

My friend, you are an inspiration to me.

To be good is not enough when you dream of being great

Cheer
Cry
Vomit
Bitch
Hope

Sterling Publishing • Meredith Press • Oxmoor House • Rodale Press • Good Housekeeping • Women's Day • Family Circle • Creative Ideas For Living • CM. Offray • Baskin Robins • Michael & Co. • Simplicity Pattern Co. • McCall's Pattern Co. • Phoenix Design • Paragon Press • UN. Bucilla • Dimension • Jan Lynn • Time Life • IVP • Andrews & McMeel • Sunrise Greeting Cards • Sylvestri • Impulse Wear • Leisure Arts D...

• The Vanessa-Ann Collection •
• Chapelle Ltd. • Ivy's Garden •
• Lisa Scott • J.J. Ogden •
• Portfolio Graphics •

This is the
end of the past

spring
NINETEEN HUNDRED NINETY-SEVEN

Happiness
is not
a state to
arrive at,
but a
manner
of
traveling.

other covers & bindings

angel cover

materials
Binder: 3-ring
Foam board: 3" x 5"
Greeting card: coordinating
Paper: decorative, coordinating, 12" x 12"; translucent,
    Japanese, 24" x 36"

general supplies & tools
Craft knife
Glue: découpage
Marker: permanent
Paintbrush
Pencil
Scissors: craft
Sponge: small

instructions

1. Using craft scissors, cut out artwork from card.

2. Dilute découpage glue in a 1:1 ratio with water. Apply glue to binder cover.

3. Apply translucent paper to binder cover and gently press with damp sponge. Let project dry thoroughly. Repeat process once more.

4. Using craft knife, cut design to correspond to artwork from foam board, if desired. Apply glue to foam board. Wrap foam board with small piece of decorative paper.

5. Using pencil, write saying on scrap piece of decorative paper. Using desired color of permanent marker, write saying.

6. Glue decorative pieces and artwork to binder cover.

celestial insights cover

materials
Book with blank pages: 9¼" x 9"
Charms
Greeting card: coordinating
Paper: handmade, 8" x 9"; 10¼" x 6"

general supplies & tools
Adhesive
Paintbrush
Pantina green
Pen: calligraphy
Scissors: craft

instructions

1. Adhere 8" x 9" handmade paper diagonally across front cover of book. Tear and adhere 10¼" x 6" handmade paper to cover portion of 8" x 9" handmade paper.

2. Wrap paper around back binding of book, and fold piece over top edge of book to inside front cover. Adhere to secure.

3. Using craft scissors, cut out artwork from card. Glue artwork over 8" x 9" paper on lower right corner of book.

4. Using paintbrush and pantina green, apply over charms to antique. Adhere charms on front of book as desired.

5. Using calligraphy pen, write saying on 8" x 9" handmade paper.

Save anything from private thoughts to favorite family recipes to much loved photographs in this scrapbook. Match the greeting card to the subject.

simple appliqué cover

materials
Album: cardboard, ring binder
Double-sided fusible web
Fabric: muslin; coordinating cotton; assorted
    coordinating scraps

general supplies & tools
Iron/ironing board
Markers: permanent #05 black
Ruler
Scissors: fabric

instructions
1. Measure an opened, flat album. Add 1" to height and width measurements and cut piece from muslin fabric. Cut two pieces of muslin ⅛" smaller than inside cover.

2. Measure and cut a strip of cotton fabric 2⅛" wider and 1" longer than spine.

3. Refer to General Instructions for **Tea-dying** on page 18. Tea-dye muslin, cotton and fabric scraps. Press fabrics after tea-dying

4. Refer to General Instructions for **Fusible Appliqué** on page 15. Reduce or enlarge **Simple Shapes Pattern** on page 114. Trace motifs onto paper side of fusible web. Cut around motifs. Iron motifs to back sides of fabric scraps. Cut out motifs.

5. Apply fusible web to back side of muslin cover, cotton spine, and inside cover pieces. Refer to **Diagram 1** below. Remove paper backing and iron muslin onto album cover, wrapping edges to inside of cover. Iron cotton spine fabric in place, wrapping ends to inside of cover and clipping as necessary to fit around ring hardware. Iron inside cover pieces to inside front and back covers to hide raw edges.

6. Iron motifs onto front and back cover as shown in photo.

7. Draw stitch lines around edges of motifs and spine fabric using a black permanent marker.

Diagram 1

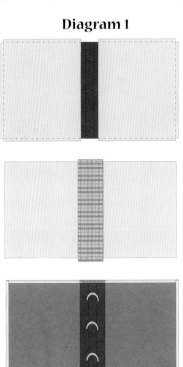

paper around left end of text papers for binding and punch holes as in Step 2.

4. Using textile ink, randomly stamp buildings on wire-edge ribbon and around top and bottom edge of scrapbook cover.

5. Using alphabet stamps, stamp book title on top center of journal cover.

6. Thread ribbon through holes and tie into a bow.

home sweet binding

materials
Cardstock: coordinating, 8½" x 11"
Paper: corrugated; medium-weight text
Ribbon: 1½"-wide coordinating wire-edge
Stamps: alphabet, small buildings
Textile ink

general supplies & tools
Paper punch
Scissors: craft, fabric

instructions
1. Using craft scissors, cut cardstock paper in half.

2. Punch two holes in left end of both pieces of cardstock, ¼" from edge and 1" from top and bottom edges.

3. Cut text paper to 8¼" x 5". Evenly fold corrugated

string binding

materials
Cardboard: lightweight
Paper: corrugated; medium-weight text
Thread: binding

general supplies & tools
Adhesive

Awl
Craft knife
Mallet
Needle
Ruler: metal edge

instructions

1. Trim medium-weight text paper to desired page size using a craft knife and ruler.

2. Trim lightweight cardboard to fit as a cover around text papers. Trim corrugated paper same size as cardboard. Adhere corrugated paper to top side of cardboard cover.

3. Refer to General Instructions for **Scoring** on page 18. Measure and mark width of spine on inside cover and gently score. Fold cover to fit around text paper.

4. Mark the position of binding holes. Top and bottom holes should be ⅝" from top and bottom edges and 1" from spine edge. Two remaining holes should be spaced equal distances in between top and bottom holes. Pierce holes with an awl and mallet.

5. Thread needle and knot end of thread. Turn book face down and insert needle up through text paper and out at second hole from right, hiding knotted string end inside text pages. Bring needle around spine to front of book and up again through same hole. Tightly pull thread. Continue stitching as shown in **Diagram 1 (A–L)**.

6. Return to original hole and bring needle around stitching as though picking up a thread. Pull thread tightly into a knot.

Diagram 1

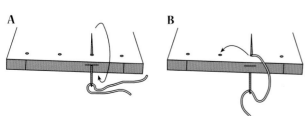

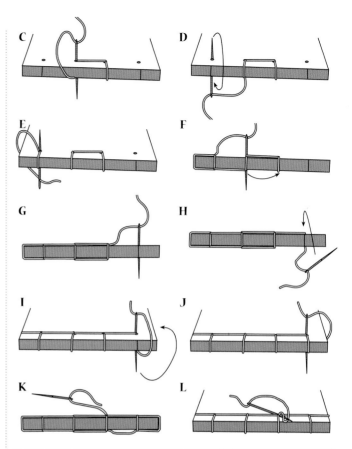

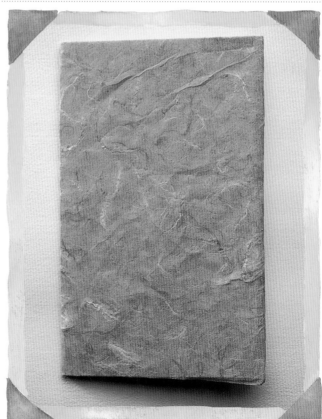

flutter binding

materials

Cardboard: lightweight
Paper: handmade textured; medium-weight text

general supplies & tools

Adhesive
Craft knife
Ruler: metal edge

instructions

1. Trim lightweight cardboard to desired book size using a craft knife and ruler. Trim handmade textured paper ¼" larger than cardboard. Trim medium-weight text paper same height as cardboard and ½" wider than width of cardboard.

2. Apply adhesive to one side of cardboard and adhere handmade textured paper to cardboard, wrapping and adhering excess edges to back side of cardboard, to form book cover. Fold book cover in half.

3. Refer to General Instructions for **Scoring** on page 18. Measure ½" from one short end of text paper and score. Fold scored edge up to form a flap as shown in **Diagram 1**. Repeat process for desired number of pages.

4. With flap side of paper facing down, fold opposite end of paper over to meet folded edge and crease in half. Repeat process for remaining papers.

5. Stack folded papers with flaps facing upward. Apply adhesive to flap on bottom paper and adhere next paper in stack to adhesive flap as shown in **Diagram 2**. Repeat process for remaining papers.

6. Adhere edge of bottom paper and top flap to inside edges of book cover as shown in **Diagram 3**.

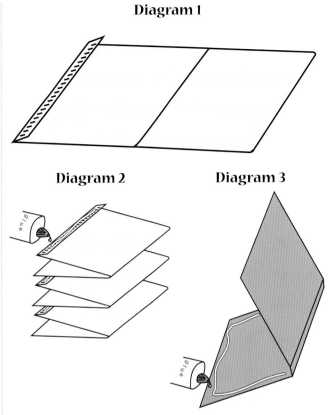

Diagram 1

Diagram 2   **Diagram 3**

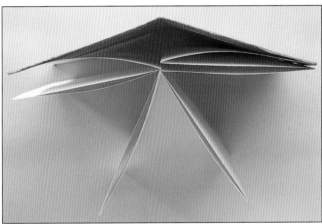

Flutter Binding (top view)

Receipt Book Binding (top view)   See page 118

receipt book binding

materials
Cardboard, lightweight : 3" x 3⅛", 3⅛" x 8½" (2)
Cording
Paper: 6¼" x 15" medium weight text (30)
Thread: heavyweight

general supplies & tools
Adhesive
Awl
Craft knife
Mallet
Needle
Ruler: metal edge

instructions
1. Fold papers in half lengthwise. Make three stacks of ten papers. Fold each stack in half, short end to short end, and crease fold as shown in **Diagram 1**.

2. Fold small cardboard piece in half lengthwise. Apply adhesive to inside of cardboard and adhere to spine of one stack of papers as shown in **Diagram 2** for center section of book.

3. Fold one short end of large cardboard pieces over ½". Apply adhesive to inside of ½" sections and adhere to spines of remaining stacks of papers, making certain one cardboard piece faces up for front cover and one faces down for back cover, and all folded edges of papers are at top.

4. Open center section to middle and place face down on work surface. Pierce two holes ½" from top and bottom edges using an awl and mallet. Thread cording through holes as shown in **Diagram 3**.

5. Close center section and place between front and back covers as shown in **Diagram 4**. Open to middle of front and back sections and place face down on work surface. Pierce two holes through all sections ⅜" from top and bottom edges. Thread heavyweight thread through holes and tightly tie into a knot.

6. Close sections into a book. Tie cording into a knot at spine. Knot ends together as shown in **Diagram 5**. Decorate cover as desired.

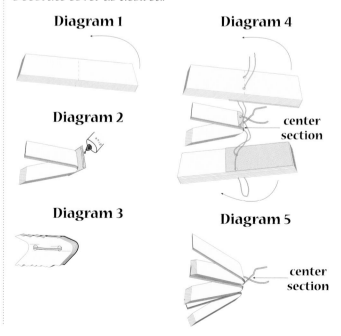

Diagram 1

Diagram 2

Diagram 3

Diagram 4

center
section

Diagram 5

center
section

3. Trim one sheet of paper ¼" larger than cardboard. Thin adhesive with water 1:1 and brush onto paper. Center and adhere outside cover to paper. Turn book over and gently smooth paper, wrapping excess paper to inside of cover.

4. Trim one sheet of paper ¼" smaller than inside cover. Brush adhesive onto paper. Adhere paper to inside of cover to cover raw edges.

5. Trim remaining papers ⅛" smaller than cover. Stack papers and lay on opened inside cover.

6. Pierce binding holes in center of spine using an awl beginning and ending 1" from top and bottom edges.

7. Thread cording through needle and sew a double running stitch down and back up through binding holes as shown in **Diagram 1 (A–E)**. Twist end of cording around top inside stitch and secure with adhesive

flower paper binding

materials

Cardboard: heavy-weight
Cording: ⅛"-wide coordinating
Paper: handmade flower (8)

general supplies & tools

Adhesive
Awl
Craft knife
Needle: large-eyed
Ruler: metal edge

instructions

1. Trim cardboard to desired book size using a craft knife and ruler.

2. Mark desired width for spine on inside cover and score.

Diagram 1

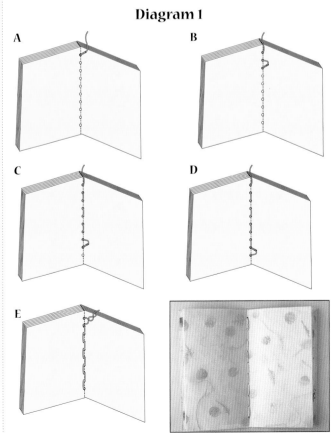

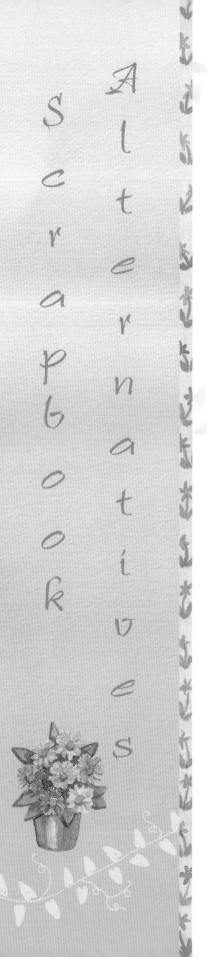

japanese cookbook

materials
Book with blank pages: 9" x 5¾"
Cardstock: 2 sheets
Chop sticks: 1 set
Die-cut: decorative, large

general supplies & tools
Glue: craft
Pen: fine-point, permanent

instructions
1. Adhere cardstock to front and back covers of book, wrapping edges to inside covers.

2. Glue decorative die-cut on front of book.

3. Refer to **"Recipe" Pattern** at right. Using pen, write Japanese characters on front of book, or substitute words in the language of the country the food originates from.

4. Glue chopsticks onto front of book.

120

materials

Acrylic paint: coordinating
Buttons: silver orb, 1⅛"-wide (4)
Cardstock: coordinating
Cigar box: 7" x 8½"
Greeting cards: 4–5
Oil pastel crayons: coordinating (2)
Photographs: 1–2
Stickers

general supplies & tools

Acrylic gesso
Acrylic spray sealer
Craft knife
Glue: craft; industrial-strength
Markers: medium-point, permanent (2)
Paintbrush
Paper towels
Pencil
Plastic wrap
Toothbrush

instructions

1. Apply acrylic gesso to inside and outside of box.

2. Using acrylic paint, basecoat outside of box.

3. Using a square piece of plastic wrap crumpled into a ball, dip into acrylic paint and wipe excess onto paper towel. Randomly sponge onto top and sides of box.

4. Using toothbrush and acrylic paint, splatter top and sides of box.

5. Refer to **Diamond Pattern**. Using cardstock and craft knife, cut out pattern.

6. Using diamond pattern and oil pastel crayons, draw diamonds onto all four sides of box. Brush off excess oil pastel.

7. Using marker, draw lines around diamond patterns. Repeat process with different color marker.

8. Arrange greeting cards, photographs, and stickers as desired onto box. Using pencil, trace around each, then remove. Apply thin layer of craft glue to back side of cards and photographs. Reposition onto cigar box lid. Attach stickers as desired. Spray box with sealer.

9. Using industrial-strength glue, position and glue buttons to bottom corners of box.

Diamond Pattern

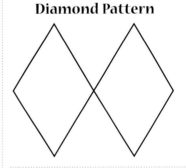

A box decorated and filled with tea and pastry recipes and tea party pictures is a sweet bridal shower gift!

Clip newspaper articles pertaining to school events (or use programs from school plays, school bulletins, or award certificates) and create a collage. Copy collage at a copy center. Mount photos on copy as desired.

Certificate of Award

Miss Drill Team Utah Pageant

This certificate has been awarded to

Devery Ferrin

for outstanding participation

for the year 1993

Devery Ferrin

STANDARD
EXAMINER
FUNDRAISER
RACE 5 K

ST. GEORGE
MARATHON
1993
10TH PLACE

ST. GEORGE MARATHON
October 2, 1993
Marathon Foto

TRACK AND
CROSSCOUNTRY

LETTERED

OGDEN HIGH SCHOOL

BOYS AND GIRLS TRACK REGION CHAMPIONS

OGDEN HIGH SCHOOL
1892 CENTENNIAL 1992

Devery Ferrin

Ogden City Schools.

PRE-TEST

POST-

Certificate of Achievement

Presented by the Board of Education of Ogden City

Certificate Of Achievement

Presented To

Devery Ferrin

FOR OUTSTANDING ACHIEVEMENT IN

EARLY COLLEGE
WEBER STATE UNIVERSITY

SCIENCE FAIR
SUPERIOR AND STATE
SUPERIOR WINNER
1988

SCIENCE FAIR
SWEEPSTAKES
WINNER
1989

Sari Vanessa Buehler

**PRESIDENT'S
LEADERSHIP
COUNCIL
SCHOLARSHIP**

LEADERSHIP

Senior officers

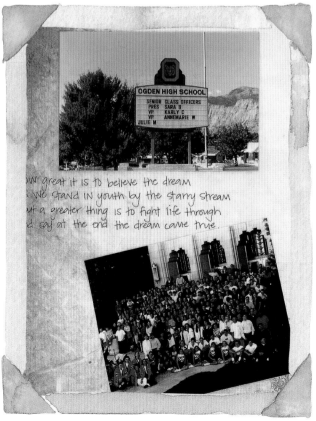

ow great it is to believe the dream
We stand in youth by the starry stream
ut a greater thing is to fight life through
d say at the end the dream came true.

memories shadow box

materials

Acrylic paint: coordinating (2)
Brads: ¾" metal (4)
Embellishments: framed photograph;
    greeting cards; dried flowers; doily;
    buttons; charms
Glass: ⅛" thick, 12¾" x 10½"
Hinges: (2)
Magnets: ¾" diameter (2)
Paper: wrapping
Wood: ¼"-thick plywood, 13" x 12½";
    ¾"-thick plywood, 9" x 18"; block, 1" square

general supplies & tools

Acrylic gesso
Clamps: large (4)
Chisel
Crackle medium
Glue: découpage, antique finish; hot glue gun
    and glue sticks; wood
Paintbrush
Pencil
Router
Sandpaper: medium-grit
Scissors: craft
Stain: fruitwood
Table saw

Instructions

1. Using table saw, cut two 1½" x 12½" pieces for shadow box sides, two 1½" x 10" pieces for shadow box sides, and one 11" x 12½" piece for shadow box back, from ¼" plywood.

2. Using clamps and wood glue, glue sides and back of shadow box together. Check to make certain all pieces are squared. Let glue dry thoroughly. Using medium-grit sandpaper, sand all edges of box.

3. Cut two 2" x 16" and two 2" x 14" pieces from ¾" plywood for frame. Miter corners at 45° angle.

4. Using clamps and wood glue, glue frame pieces together. Check to make certain all pieces are squared.

5. Using router, cut ¼"-wide x ⁵⁄₁₆"-deep groove around inside edge of frame for glass placement. Using a chisel, remove round corners.

6. Using craft scissors, cut wrapping paper to fit inside shadow box back.

7. Apply acrylic gesso to inside of shadow box and frame.

8. Using acrylic paint, basecoat inside of shadow box and frame.

9. Apply crackle medium to frame. Using acrylic paint, apply topcoat, in contrasting color, to frame.

10. Apply stain to inside of shadow box and frame.

11. Sand all edges of frame for antique appearance.

12. Using antique finish découpage glue, découpage wrapping paper to inside shadow box back.

13. Attach shadow box to frame with hinges.

14. Place and secure glass in frame using one brad in each corner of frame.

15. Using wood glue, glue one magnet to frame. Glue other magnet to 1" square wood block. Glue block to box side with magnet side up, touching magnet on frame.

16. Using craft scissors, cut front from greeting card. Trim card as desired. Using hot glue gun and glue stick, embellish shadow box as desired.

Pictured at right is a variation on the theme of this shadow box. Gather momentos from a special outing and save them in a green shadow box.

framed box

materials
Brads: ¾" metal (8–12)
Fabric: low pile velvet, 13"–19" square (2)
Frame, with 10½" x 12½" opening for lid
Glass: ⅛" thick single strength, to fit frame
Grosgrain ribbon: coordinating 2"
Mat board: 13"–18" square
Wood moulding: similar to, but wider than
    frame moulding

general supplies & tools
Craft knife
Glue: craft, industrial strength epoxy, wood
Hammer
Ruler
Saw
Scissors: craft
Spray adhesive
Stain: to match frame
Staple gun and staples

Instructions
1. Using ruler, measure outside edges of frame to be used for a lid to determine box size. Add a little to each box side measurement to allow for mitered corners, depending on moulding shape. (The rabbet of the moulding must be slightly larger than outside edges of

the lid so the lid will sit in the rabbet of the box moulding.)

2. Using these measurements and allowing for miters, cut the moulding into four pieces of the correct length using saw. Miter corners at 45° angle. Cut the moulding so that the rabbet edge is upright and the front face of the moulding is the side of the box.

3. Using wood glue, secure moulding pieces together to form box sides. Strengthen as needed with brads.

4. Stain both sides of moulding to finish box sides. Let dry.

5. Cut mat board to same dimension as outside edges of box sides. Cut one piece of fabric to dimension of mat board. Adhere to one side of mat board using spray adhesive. Secure edges using a fine bead of craft glue. Cut remaining piece of fabric one inch larger on all sides than dimensions of mat board. Place fabric face down on a flat surface. Coat plain side of mat board with spray adhesive. Center mat board with sprayed side down on larger piece of fabric. Wrap and secure fabric edges to previously covered side of mat board using a fine bead of craft glue.

6. Staple covered mat board to bottom edges of box sides with raw edges of fabric meeting the wood.

7. Position frame face down on a flat surface. Run a very fine continuous bead of industrial strength epoxy along rabbet. Place glass in frame, forming a lid. Allow epoxy to dry.

8. Fold grograin ribbon in half and secure ends together with craft glue. Center and glue raw ends of ribbon to inside edge of one short side of lid so ribbon protrudes from lid for a handle.

9. Place lid to rest in rabbet of moulding box.

flower girl

materials
Paper: handmade floral
Pressed dried flowers and leaves
Ribbon: ⅛"-wide coordinating (3)

general supplies & tools
Adhesive
Craft knife

instructions
1. Carefully peel up small floral pieces in handmade paper using a craft knife.

2. Slip photograph under floral pieces and adhere to paper. Adhere floral pieces to photograph.

3. Hold ribbons together as one and tie into a bow around dried flowers and leaves. Adhere flowers to paper. Frame as desired.

between each. Use a torn sheet of paper as stencil and deepest color of paint to create ragged edge sponging effect. Stamp over sponging using deepest color of paint and three or four different rubber stamps. Draw details with fine line metallic marker. Punch holes along sealed side of envelope to match binder.

stamped envelope

Turn a manilla envelope into a scrapbook page that can also hold loose phototgraphs. Choose three colors of acrylic paint. Sponge on each color separately, drying

metric conversion chart

mm-millimetres   cm-centimetres
inches to millimetres and centimetres

inches	mm	cm	inches	cm	inches	cm
⅛	3	0.3	9	22.9	30	76.2
¼	6	0.6	10	25.4	31	78.7
½	13	1.3	12	30.5	33	83.8
⅝	16	1.6	13	33.0	34	86.4
¾	19	1.9	14	35.6	35	88.9
⅞	22	2.2	15	38.1	36	91.4
1	25	2.5	16	40.6	37	94.0
1¼	32	3.2	17	43.2	38	96.5
1½	38	3.8	18	45.7	39	99.1
1¾	44	4.4	19	48.3	40	101.6
2	51	5.1	20	50.8	41	104.1
2½	64	6.4	21	53.3	42	106.7
3	76	7.6	22	55.9	43	109.2
3½	89	8.9	23	58.4	44	111.8
4	102	10.2	24	61.0	45	114.3
4½	114	11.4	25	63.5	46	116.8
5	127	12.7	26	66.0	47	119.4
6	152	15.2	27	68.6	48	121.9
7	178	17.8	28	71.1	49	124.5
8	203	20.3	29	73.7	50	127.0

index

acid..................................18
acid & lignin free paper.........19
acid free.............................19
acid free paper....................19
acid migration.....................19
adhesives...........................8
albums 8
alternatives to plastic page
    protectors 22
alternatives to traditional
    scrabooks.....................22
angel cover.......................111
angel house.......................63
antiquity............................85
archiving...........................18
archival quality....................18
archival terms......................18
art of marriage....................81
assembling clues from
    the past........................24
baby book.........................49
baby bundle.......................33
baby in black & white.....49–51
baby pages.....................50–51
beginning with safe photograph
    handling, a theme, and a
    color scheme..................7
binders.............................8
black & white vs. color.........29
buffered paper.....................19
buffering...........................19
bunny hop..........................55
butterfly kisses...................63
calculating page
    measurements................7
camera angles....................27
camera viewfinders..............27
causes of red eye................28
celestial insights cover........112
chemical stability.................19
choosing from available
    scrapbook supplies..........8
circle cutter........................8
clip art..............................8
color wheel........................8
cordially invited..................79
corner rounders...................9
corner templates..................9
correct image cropping.........27
correcting red eye...............28
cotton or linen paper............19
craft knife..........................9
craft punches......................9
craft scissors......................9
creating albums just for fun....21

creating an archival quality
    scrapbook.....................20
crimper.............................9
critter quiz........................45
'crop'..............................14
cropping photographs..........12
corrugator.........................9
cutting metal......................14
daddy's coat......................36
daughter's dreams........59–67
days gone by......................96
dear friends.....................101
decorative edge scissors........9
découpage.........................14
die cuts.............................9
displaying family histories......27
don'ts..............................12
embossing copper...............14
embossing paper.................15
embossing powder...............11
embossing stencils...............9
enhancements....................12
envelope keepers................65
fabric through the year...52–58
fabric photo mat.................50
family history......................24
family quilt........................86
family tree.........................66
federal records...................25
filling in the gaps................24
film tips............................28
finding acid-free scrapbook
    supplies........................21
flower girl........................126
flower paper binding...........119
flutter binding...................117
fold-out pets......................43
framed box.......................125
fuschia frames....................93
fusible appliqué..................15
garter photo corners............82
general information......6–29
generations.......................79
grandma's fan....................91
great-grandma....................51
halloween.........................38
handmade paper ovals..........16
hand-tinting photographs......16
happy birthday...................34
heat-coloring metal.............16
heat tool..........................11
high school days.................68
highschool highlights.....68–75
high school pages................69
holiday stocking..................41
home sweet binding...........115

interactive pop-up
    pictures...................30–42
improving photographs.........27
introduction........................6
japanese cookbook...........120
laws associated with records...27
lettering...........................13
lettering booklets.................9
light box............................9
lignin free paper..................19
little sister.........................98
local records......................25
marbling paper....................16
markers.............................10
memorabilia—what to save....13
memories shadow box.......124
mother & daughter............103
motivation..........................6
mylar...............................19
novelty edge rulers..............10
organdy envelope................88
organizing supplies..............13
oriental lace.....................103
other covers & bindings..111–119
other sources......................26
outdoor photographs...........28
pansy border......................98
paper...............................10
paper cutter.......................10
paper terms.......................19
passion for pets.............43–48
pencils.............................10
pens...............................10
permanent paper................19
pet pages......................44–48
pet profile.........................46
pH testing pen....................10
photo corners.....................10
photo frames......................10
photo journaling..................13
photo labeling pencil...........11
photo labs.........................29
photographic restoration......29
photography.......................27
picture pop-up....................30
pigment ink pads................11
plastic terms......................19
plastic wrap painting...........17
pocket pages......................13
poetry & lace.....................81
polypropylene.....................19
polyethylene......................19
pretty package....................57
preventing red eye...............28
pumpkin patch...................56
receipt book binding..........118
red eye pen........................11

removing photographs from self
    adhesive albums.............21
researching family history......24
ribbon & lace...............85–95
ribbon embroidery...............18
ribbon flowers....................51
rubber stamps....................11
safe scrapbook storage........23
saving non-archival
    memorabilia..................21
school lunch......................39
scoring.............................18
scrapbook alternatives.120–128
scrapbooking.......................6
seasons............................52
sentimental journey....108–110
sentimental pages.............108
shane game.......................47
sheet protectors..................11
ship...............................100
simple appliqué cover.........113
sister's favorite...................95
special awards..................121
special delivery.................102
special techniques...............14
sponging paper...................18
spray neutralizer.................11
stamped envelope.............127
stencils.............................11
stickers.............................12
string binding....................115
start at home.....................24
state records......................25
storing negatives................22
storing photographs on
    CD-ROM.......................23
sunflower pocket.................37
tea-dyeing........................18
templates..........................11
textured treasures........96–107
textured pages...........97–107
theme packets & kits............12
title page...........................45
to my daughter..................59
tradition...........................46
train...............................99
transferring.......................18
treasure box.....................121
trellis...............................94
trimmers...........................10
valentine...........................54
victorian house...................82
wedding album...................76
wedding pages...................77
weddings past....................77
weddings vows...................90
weddings are forever.....76–84